M000018970

BECOME
THE
SUCCESSFUL
COACH
YOU ARE MEANT TO BE

Become the Successful Coach You Are Meant to Be

Copyright © 2018 by Feroshia Knight | Coach Training World

All rights reserved.

No portion of this book may be reproduced by any electronic or mechanical means or used in any manner without written permission from the author, except for use by a reviewer for brief quotations within a book review.

For worldwide distribution.

This book is a product of the author's experience and opinions. It is sold with the understanding that the author and publisher are not distributing specific career counseling or advice. Neither the author nor the publisher assume responsibility for errors, inaccuracies or omissions and claim no responsibility or liability whatsoever for the use, application or interpretation of the material contained within this publication. Reader assumes full responsibility for the use of information in this book.

First Edition: May 2018

ISBN 978-1-7322238-0-6

In memory of Daniel Powers, who left us far too soon.
May your brilliant wings fly high in the sky above.

Acknowledgements

As every writer knows, a project like this could never become a reality without the contributions, sacrifice and support of others. In more than two decades serving individuals and businesses as a professional coach and coach trainer, my thank-you list far exceeds even the voluminous space available on the Internet. But there are a few who stand out.

I would like to express my deepest gratitude to the coaching community as a whole. You have been a constant light, shining far brighter than I had ever dreamed. To the graduates of Coach Training World, and specifically the coaches featured within this work, I also give my heartfelt appreciation. Your unique adaptations of Whole Person Coaching are a daily source of inspiration to me for what they provide to others: connection, courage and commitment. The world needs more changemakers like you!

My thanks also to Molokai and Kumi for their enduring, unconditional love, and waiting patiently while I worked on this book, their little noses pressed to the windowpanes as countless smells passed them by. It's done – let's go for a walk!

To Ryan May, my right hand in the process, I'm glad beyond words to have you as my collaborator and co-conspirator. As a woman who is far more comfortable speaking than writing, the support you've provided has been priceless.

And finally, my many thanks to you, dear reader. You've landed in the right place. As any coach will tell you, this is more than just a profession – it's a calling. So to you, who have taken the first (and often hardest) step toward answering that call, I offer my applause, support and solemn pledge: your best life is just ahead.

Author's Note

The stories and examples shared herein are taken from real people who, in many cases, braved a great deal to overcome their personal stopping blocks and move toward their best life – one suited uniquely to them and, more importantly, of their own choosing.

Most of the names used in this book are those of the individuals themselves, provided with their kind permission. But in some cases, names, identifying details and other specifics have been slightly modified to respect the privacy of those wishing to protect certain aspects of their lives, their family or their clients.

A heartfelt thanks to one and all: you've made this book what it is.

Table of Contents

Introduction

How did you get to where you are today? How did you end up holding this book in your hands? And how did you make the decision to take steps toward the personal and professional development these choices represent?

As we move through life, each step we take is the result of choice. Our choices – ranging from what we should have for lunch to where we live and how we intend to spend the rest of our lives – all begin with a series of questions reflective of our needs and desires in that moment.

These questions are simple, and often answered before the questions themselves have a chance to fully form within our minds. Nevertheless, they provide a powerful source of direction for our daily living. Even more significantly, these seemingly small choices have a broad, cumulative effect. They greatly impact the course of our lives and run the gamut from health to happiness.

What are the choices you have made in your life up to this point? Have they led you to a place of life-fulfillment, prosperity and balance? Do you enjoy a career or business you truly love? Are you fulfilled in your relationships? Does your life reflect the person you want to be? Or are you standing at a crossroads, feeling lost and disconnected from yourself, others and your life, wondering which way to go?

If you fall into the latter category, or just happen to be somewhere outside of where you'd really like to be, I've got some inspiring news: you are only a few choices away from a preferred future, career and business your future self will thank you for.

This book is all about making a difference. Your difference, in fact! The coaching industry is unique in that it offers unlimited applications and options for personalization. As a professional coach, you can make your inimitable difference in the lives and businesses of others, as only you can, simply by being YOU.

Unlike other career tracks, you can fully customize your offerings within several popular coaching niches. You'll fashion your services entirely around your unique personality, passionate interests, life experience and the wisdom you've earned throughout life – both personally and professionally.

In case you're wondering, you have a tribe out there right now, just waiting for you to arrive. While other career tracks attempt to suppress or even penalize you for your goals, financial expectations, and even certain aspects of your personality, your tribe is actively seeking you out for this combination of heartfelt drive and brilliance. That's the beauty of the coaching industry:

you get to bring your whole self to work. You are only limited by your imagination.

Becoming a professional coach also allows you to bring all your experience into your new life-changing career. In other words, you don't have to start over. You are simply building upon your prior experience and stepping into a career or business that is truly representative of your greatest potential.

What is the origin of this book?

Every superhero has an origin story. You are building the foundations of yours at this very moment. Mine is contained within this book. It's the product of nearly three decades of experience in the business of change. It encompasses the tools and lessons learned from my days as an introverted, behind-the-scenes business and marketing strategist. And it extends all the way through my experience as a Whole Person Coach and global teacher who has helped thousands of changemakers and entrepreneurs in various phases of their personal- and business-growth journeys. Side by side, I've shown individuals throughout the world, and from all walks of life, how to step into the light and be treasured for the true value they can offer their clients and the world as a whole.

My accumulated wisdom is derived from my own journey, as well as those around me. As you'll see, my life and business experience have served me as key spiritual teachers. The journeys taken by those in my outstanding global tribe of changemakers have also given my work deep meaning, and me a sense of immense fulfillment.

This book began as a simple concept: how to become a coach and create a rewarding, life-fulfilling and sustainable business. But as the pages filled, I realized there was far more to being a treasured changemaker than just a sustainable business model, marketing strategy, and professional change-mastery skills. The success of your own life-changing business is as much about your capacity to learn, grow and change, as it is about your clients. At the core of this work is your capacity to overcome doubt and create inner peace inside the frequently immense discomfort of change.

For decades people would poke fun at my name, "Feroshia," inquiring if I was ferocious. But if they could have seen how much I doubted my own self on the inside, maybe they'd have thought twice about cracking wise. The surface of the ocean is unreflective of what lies just beneath the water line. Isn't it ironic?

I've spent decades mastering the art, science and business of transformation. I took the long road. You don't have to. It is my deepest wish that, as a fellow treasured changemaker, you can light the way faster and more efficiently – because your audience needs you now. And last but not least: you too can face whatever holds you back and step forward into the life you are meant to live.

How is this book different?

When you purchased this book, you gave me your trust. Trust is the most valuable gift anyone can give someone else, so I don't treat that lightly. As your guide for the next few hundred pages, and a transformational coach in the business of change, I promise to spend our time together wisely.

My mission is your success. This book is different for many reasons, but three in particular:

Difference #1: You'll know what to do and what not to do; enabling you to save money, time and effort.

I am a serial entrepreneur and veteran in the business of change. I have a thirty-year track record of inventing and reinventing my dream-come-true business, focused intensely on marketing, sales and transformation. As with any greater luminary, I know both the light and dark parts of starting and succeeding in the business of change.

There are no templates, marketing strategies or business-building plans that can fit everyone's unique experience – especially one that leverages the digital domain to access the global marketplace. So I'm here to impart what works and what doesn't, saving you (and enabling you to save others in turn) from the costly mistakes that can discourage and derail progress.

Difference #2: You'll be learning from someone who has mastered both ends of the spectrum!

As the field of coaching continues to burgeon, you'll find no shortage of "coaches" teaching people how to become coaches, and even more people teaching coaches how to market their services. Unfortunately, very few of these individuals have marketed themselves as coaches working from the ground up. Even fewer have helmed coach training programs or schools and developed their own brand, marketing strategy, and sustainable business model exclusively in the business of change.

As an ICF-accredited Master Certified Coach (MCC), my journey includes growing and sustaining two private coaching businesses and an international coach training institute. I've personally trained well over a thousand coaches and worked with hundreds of successful businesses in a variety of specialties. So I know the path well. In addition, I pride myself on staying current with the digital age coaching has now entered. This includes programs and products, as well as online marketing. I can't wait to share the road of new media with you and show you how easy it is to prosper on your own terms. My mission is to ensure more people like you bring their whole self to life, so they in turn can influence others to do the same.

Liberation is the name of the game. Change mastery is the key.

Difference #3: You'll have the whole picture.

You'll not only know how to transform lives, but how to leverage your strengths, skills and unique personality to create your own one-of-a-kind coaching business. I'm a comprehensive, detail-oriented gal. Over the years, I've found that if you want to coach, transform and prosper, you need to develop and master skills both in coaching and business development.

Trust me, both sides of the business can be deeply creative and rewarding with the proper mentality and commitment. In fact, modern science demonstrates anything can be learned with the right mindset, a fair amount of devotion, and a good mentor who is willing to help you do it your way. SPOILER ALERT: that's going to be the secret to your success as a coach in a nutshell.

The power of relationship

The fields of interpersonal neurobiology, psychology and related sciences clearly demonstrate the highly beneficial (dare we say 'game-changing') qualities that result from supportive partnerships and interactions with others in all aspects of life. This is especially true of creativity, innovation, personal success and happiness.

That's where you come in.

As a Whole Person Coach, regardless of your specialty or niche focus, the co-creative process you offer your clients engages them to draw upon their own resources and step into their wholeness. In doing so, they accelerate their ability to learn and grow through the process.

Your experience and expertise fuel your ability to be a highly adept collaborator and resourceful partner. Offering thought-provoking, often pivotal questions, you light the way for others as you elicit the insights and inspiration your clients need to succeed.

Throughout this process, your clients unlock their already present potential. You champion them to holistically leverage their whole selves, generating strategic actions vital to creating their desired outcomes. Within the coaching relationship, you continue to fluidly motivate your clients along their chosen pathway. You help them leverage their very best, all the way to the finish line, and always in direct alignment with their agenda.

The result? Your clients reach their goals. Better yet, they do so while developing the capacity to be "self-innovative." This is by far one of the biggest takeaways of the Whole Person Coaching relationship, and one we will examine in detail later on. But for now, simply know that self-innovation enables someone to learn the life-mastery skills innate in coaching. It primes them to create or manage change in any aspect of their life… and for the rest of their life!

Success stories

Nothing is more inspiring to me than someone who succeeds at a goal they've set for themselves by leveraging the power of coaching – especially when they exceed their own expectations. Just thinking about some of my former students brings tears of joy as I've witnessed them changing the world in their own unique ways!

The case studies you'll find in this book are real people (both students and clients) who did what it took to achieve their dreams and show up whole in their inner and outer arenas. The impressive results they earn each day come from a willingness to be open to fresh perspectives and innovative approaches. Over the years, we've laughed, cried, and at times screamed for joy at both the trials and triumphs that come from being a changemaker, entrepreneur and whole person.

These are people deeply committed to their success and that of their clients. Their results were driven by what mattered most to them: their core values, their own needs, and being at the top of their economic engine. I am so tremendously proud of what they've achieved. This book would be an empty shell without the encouragement they provide.

This inspiration is compounded by the fact that they started exactly where you are right now. If you are willing to learn (which also means unlearning at times) and can be both patient and determined, you will create your dream-come-true coaching business, reshaping your life and future into anything you desire. You are limited only by the depth and breadth of your aspirations.

My journey

At a very young age, I perplexed the adults around me. Instead of opening a lemonade stand and dancing around on the side of a busy street to flag cars down, I spent countless hours making "how-to" booklets. My first product was a book of mazes and crossword puzzles. Later, I expanded my publishing repertoire to include miniature how-to books, teaching the secrets of kitchen gadgets. I especially loved drawing each gadget, carefully labeling the components in vivid detail like a schematic. I was endlessly curious (still am), and always needed to know how and why something worked the way it did.

By the time I reached seventh grade, I had picked up photography. By college, I was teaching photography in the art and journalism departments. I was no Ansel Adams or Annie Leibovitz. But I had a knack for explaining the importance of exploring unseen perspectives and unique angles that offered the audience a different point of view. I believed creativity was all about telling a different story. Images were my language.

My first adventure into the real world as a creative was at Portland, Oregon's then fourth largest advertising agency. As an intern at Kobasic, Harris and Savage Advertising, I was thrown into several major public relations accounts including Disney, Touchstone and Paramount Pictures.

Despite my success, and the glamour and glory of working with radio, print and TV stations to get the agency's clients into the public eye, it wasn't for me. This work didn't reflect who I was – someone who wanted to make the world a better place. I was a creative, a storyteller and, unknown to me at the time, someone who wanted to have her own radius of influence.

Jobless once again, I told myself I'd find a better fit... next time. I was somewhat clear with what I wanted. But mostly I knew what I didn't want. This lack of clarity kept me in a cycle of dead-end jobs that would continue until I went to work for Richard. A kindhearted businessman, Richard saw and fully embraced my potential. Within minutes of the interview, he offered me the job of a lifetime: to wear multiple hats and be my own boss while running his business.

Richard didn't like to manage people. I didn't like to be managed. Plus, he didn't mind that my hair was platinum blonde and punkish. It was a match made in heaven. He got a loyal servant; and I found work that let me be who I was as a whole person. Within months, I was literally doing it all, immersed in my small business paradise: writing copy, shooting photos, and creating graphics, logos and just about everything from business cards to three-thousand-square-foot trade show booths. His customers loved my creative capacity to solve their problems. I loved the challenge of routinely tapping into my multiple passions and talents.

My new boss was quite happy with my capacity to take care of his customers and business. For me, nothing could have been better, that is until I learned the company was at risk of going under.

Richard was a nice guy, perhaps too nice because he was a terrible salesperson. In fact, he'd have rather made a friend, than a sale. The deep discounts he offered his clients, just to get to "yes," was now threatening my dream-come-true job. I'll never forget the plaque in his office that said: "You can either have it Fast, Good or Cheap. Pick two." Richard had mastered cheap. His employees did our best to master the other two.

Richard had become a father figure to me, so I was really invested in solving this problem. Out of desperation, I asked him if I could become an outside salesperson for the company. I had pretty much mastered everything else in the shop, sans the printing presses. (Isn't it amazing what fear can drive us to do?)

Within a few weeks, I was bringing in $10,000 to $30,000 a month in new sales. This represented substantial revenue for a new company about to go under in the 1980s. But six months later, I became disgruntled. My friends were all getting insurance at their corporate gigs. Shouldn't I? So I asked for health insurance (costing $80 a month) to cover my health, dental and vision care expenses. I can't recall which came first, the resounding "no" or the excuses reflecting his scarcity mindset. Couldn't he see I was the reason he was still in business?

I was at a crossroads once again, hurt, frustrated and divided. Should I stay, or should I go? I think you already know what happened next.

My first company Foto:Grafika, focused on portrait and product photography, quickly morphed into my second company Agent 47: Marketing & Communications. From my many passions and insatiable need to learn new things, backed by my experience working in a large agency, it seemed only natural to grow the business.

Before I knew it, I had forty-two subcontracts and was constantly adding services and talent.

Initially, I loved the work, with all its challenges and fast-paced tempo. But the stress began to slowly overwhelm me. My self-imposed workaholism fostered a general lack of life outside work. It all came to a halt with a cancer diagnosis a few years later.

Wake-up calls are actually blessings in disguise. My entire world changed within a matter of minutes. I immediately hit the pause button, as one does when life changes so rapidly. Some deep soul-searching and an abundance of personal exploration soon followed. Through supportive partnerships with various healers and guides, I found my way back to myself, rediscovering the curious inventive kid I had unknowingly left behind.

Now fully awake to my wholeness, and reconnected to my true self, I began once again to lead my life from my heart and soul. I consciously tempered my mind and its need to know. This led me to search for a new career that would reflect the whole of who I was. Creative. Curious. Compassionate. But also a pursuit that would allow me to build upon and leverage my vast experience.

This was how I discovered coaching.

Like many people I meet today, it took someone else noticing my gifts and abilities in service to others. For me, it was a client named Kyle — a senior manager in a global corporation. Recognizing his time in the corporate arena was limited, Kyle hired me to help him venture out on his own.

A few months into our working relationship, Kyle offered what is still today the most important advice I've ever received: you should become a coach.

Initially, I had no idea what Kyle was talking about – COACH? At the time, most people were only using the term in reference to sports. Curious to learn more, I started my exploration.

Within a few months, I trained to become a certified coach along with several other additional modalities I felt were missing from my training. But that's where it stalled. I didn't become a coach at that point. Instead, I fell back into old habits.

In those days, my superpower was a skillful ability to successfully market and sell other people. With each new training course or workshop I'd attend, the leaders would get wind of my marketing savvy. Next thing I knew, I was working for them to grow their businesses.

I found great rewards in supporting them to summit the top of their influence, impact and income. But it wasn't what I truly wanted to be doing. Have you ever had the feeling that everyone else is living your dream? And you are helping everybody else achieve their dreams while you remain stuck? Luckily, I recognized what was happening and shifted focus back to my dreams.

I launched my next business as a professional holistic life coach and started coaching people around work-life balance. It's funny how we do capably and willingly for others what we ourselves need most. Although I wouldn't work with cancer survivors until years later, it felt like a good first step into the health and wellness arena.

Now I don't know about you, but I'm a non-stop learner. I also love a good challenge. While I enjoyed coaching these individuals, it wasn't enough. Within the next year, I started working in the conflict arena, building upon my interests and studies in mediation and compassionate communication. What I discovered then is now the foundation of my work in Whole Person Coaching. Working inside corporations, non-profits, family-run businesses and other communities, my ability to tame tigers and heal the effects of conflict earned me a reputation... and a non-stop referral base. My high rate of success also inspired others to seek out my methodology.

So I gathered what would become my curriculum. It was derived from my own experience and expertise. I then began training others in the holistic methods I'd been using with my own clients to produce exponential results. Luckily for me, I had a wealth of contacts from my marketing agency days. Most were more than willing to have me come in and develop their leaders and teams. (The beauty of being someone who over-delivers is there will always be someone who wants you.) But it would be another five years before I would come to the realization that brought me to where I'm at today.

At this point, I must give full credit to my bestie Kim Tally. You can hear her soothing voice on some of the digital recordings in our coach training library. She has always been a steady, calm presence, even amid the most tumultuous moments in my life.

For example, while on a snowshoeing trip with Kim at Mt. Shasta, I once fell into a cavern. I was so busy complaining that my clients were not enthusiastic about my work and how frustrated I was at not being able to affect change inside a stagnant fear-fueled system, I completely missed the danger looming directly in front of me. And in I fell. Now it wasn't the Grand Canyon. But it was wide enough that I should have seen it coming.

Stuck in three feet of snow, I had nowhere to go. That's when Kim planted this one on me:

"Feroshia, you're really good at what you're doing, but you're not happy. You love teaching. You love coaching and developing others. But you're too far ahead of the times. Your clients simply aren't ready for what you've got. What if you created your own coach training methodology and trained people, just like you, who want to make the world a better place and reclaim their wholeness?"

Duh. Again, someone else showing me what I couldn't see on my own.

Baraka Institute: Leadership Development & Coach Training Center was launched in 2005, and became my first coach training school. Transitioning from the corporate and non-profit arenas, I began offering transformational change-making skills to individuals and changemakers who wanted to make their impact in their worlds of influence. A few years later, we became Coach Training World.

In the years that have passed since, I've committed myself to heart-centric, soul-driven individuals just like you! People who want to make their difference and shine their unique brilliance while earning the money they deserve. I've created businesses, products, programs and holistically-minded services that have helped countless individuals leverage their special talents to great success (and more than a little applause!).

My work has been shared with thousands of coaches who, in turn, are changing the lives of thousands more using my methods. My online marketing services and business development mentoring has helped hundreds of business owners. And today, I'm serving thousands of committed entrepreneurs with the robust courses offered through my CoachPreneur Academy business incubator.

As an ICF Master Credentialed Coach, with eleven holistic certifications and a master's degree in organizational leadership and psychology, I've helped others perfect the integrated union of personal and professional development. Among my many raving reviews, I am most proud of those given by people who appreciate my desire to address the whole business, including all the individuals operating within it.

I've also had the privilege to work alongside a diverse range of solo entrepreneurs, as well as leaders within businesses and non-profits throughout the United States, Canada, Europe and elsewhere around the world. My efforts have helped create high-impact groups in which leaders and their teams can excel at effective communication, strategic planning, decision-making, conflict management, productivity, accountability and team effectiveness.

The journey has been rich and rewarding, personally and financially. But one thing stands out above all else: I'm thankful every day for my tribe, a community of like-hearted individuals that inspire and support me as much as I strive to do the same for them. Together, our lives are truly better.

My business ventures have also provided their own spiritual teachings. They have collectively taught me valuable lessons around who I am when I'm at my best, what a treasure each moment of life is, and the rewards that come with pursuing what I absolutely love.

Three decades later, that brings me here… for you.

Your journal

As we move together through this book, I'd like you to keep a journal. It can be online or in another electronic format if you wish. A tablet might work OK, but your phone definitely won't cut it here. You've got work to do.

For the best results, I recommend writing your notes by hand. Something magical takes place in the act of putting pen to paper that we lose when we madly tap notes on a computer: reflection. So go out and invest in a large spiral-bound notebook, a composition book, or a leather-bound journal (if you're feeling particularly posh). Don't use something you have lying around the house unless it's new. A half-used, dog-earned pad with a coffee ring on the front is not the way to launch into this new phase of your life.

At the end of each chapter, you'll find prompts for your journal. These exercises cover the content from that chapter and encourage you to expand upon and personalize it to your particular goals. This is an assignment I often give to my coaching clients for one simple reason: it works.

As a prospective coach, you'll want to be familiar with what this tool can help you and your clients achieve. By chronicling your journey, you will be allowed (and encouraged) to see how your thoughts progress. You'll be amazed at how the interrelated nature of your views, feelings, actions, needs and beliefs reveal themselves on the page.

Journaling is also an excellent way to catch what is happening and come back to reflect from a fresh and often new perspective. It enables you to see yourself (and those who influence you) over time and from a bigger perspective. Plus, it feels amazing to see just how much you change and evolve – all for the better – as you take these initial steps toward becoming a professional coach.

Finally, a journal helps you develop your skills as a coach by highlighting the importance of language and how it shapes our reality. Words matter. And as you're about to learn, you must tune into them very closely to grow in your own life and help others do the same in turn.

The one thing I want to emphasize is that this is entirely for you. No one else will read it. So you should feel free to be completely open and honest. Write as much or as little as you feel. There is no pressure to fill page after page on a single exercise. However, the more thorough you are, the more insight you'll have to build on later.

Let's start right now…

~ *In Your Journal* ~

Begin your journal by writing today's date. This is your starting point (Hooray!).

Now write a few sentences detailing why you picked up this book, what you hope it will do for you, and which feelings you were experiencing when you pulled it off the shelf or bought it online.

Are you ready?

As the founder of Coach Training World, CoachPreneur Academy and creator of Whole Person Coaching, I am taking the next step in my journey with the book you're holding in your hands. This book is for you. More importantly, it's about you and your future!

If you are reading this book, I'm guessing you've had a few wake-up calls of your own. The lessons you've learned are likely serving others already in some capacity. Maybe you've traveled the road, fueling your mind and experiences with wisdom available through the myriad of psychology and self-development books, workshops and trainings. Or maybe you're just dipping your toe in the water for the first time. Wherever you're at right now, you are where you are because you're ready for change.

The road you travel in life is paved one choice at a time. It took a big wake-up call for me to finally act. But you don't have to wait for your own sign to appear. If you are in the middle of a significant life change (and the chaos and confusion that goes with it), I promise, there is already a well-paved road waiting for you. With devotion to yourself and your future, this road can land you where you want to be: one-hundred percent authentically you and helping others be at their best. If you're ready to instigate your own big shift, welcome home!

The inner voice that speaks to you – the one that keeps you awake at night or tugs at your heartstrings when you see someone who is truly alive – that's your soul calling. It's time to step forward and become the changemaker you know you can be.

Are you ready to do the work you love most and get paid what you deserve? Or will you hit the proverbial snooze button and go back to sleep? The choice is yours.

What this book can do for you

This book is geared to helping you prosper in all ways – personally and professionally – through the power of coaching.

Imagine for a moment what it would feel like to place your passionate interests, purpose and personality at the forefront of everything you do. What about a career, business and life that make it possible for you to be who you are at your best helping others? Imagine springing from bed in the morning with a fire in your soul to start the day.

If you work for others, you'll learn how to become your own boss inside your own coaching business. Instead of remaining a best-kept secret, you'll become a go-to resource who is well rewarded for your efforts, time and wisdom.

If you are already a changemaker or business owner who wants to serve more people, provide better results, and generate more income, this book has been tailor-made for you. You will discover ways to incorporate coaching into your already robust tool kit by leveraging your gifts, talents and wisdom.

And if you are like many that come to coaching in the middle of a life transition, you'll appreciate the clarity that comes from diving into this bedrock of information – not the least of which is the oasis of support available in our Facebook group:

https://www.facebook.com/groups/coachtrainingworld/

No matter what your current position, this book can transform the way you go through the world. People will be interested in hearing about your business and what you do, curious (and dare I say a little envious) as to how you set yourself free. You will have time for yourself again, time that can be invested in leisure activities, spending time with family, or aspects of self-care. Best of all, you won't be at the beck and call of someone else's business, making their dream a reality while yours sits on the back burner.

In the following pages, we'll travel the road on how to become a professional coach and successfully launch your coaching business. You'll learn exactly what you need to do to gain the clarity and confidence to seek and obtain the clients and cash you desire in the business of change.

Lastly, we'll explore some of the frequently asked questions that have arisen from those who've stood right where you are today. Just like you, they were searching for their unique niche. And like them, you're going to come out successful on the other end.

Here's to your future self!

~1~

The Changemaker You Already Are

You are the one they want

You are a bona fide rarity, possessing the experience and drive to help others succeed. In fact, you've probably been helping others all your life.

How many times have others come to you with personal or professional problems? Friends, family, coworkers, and sometimes even complete strangers share their most intimate struggles, insecurities, and stumbling blocks. These people trust your wisdom and the perspective you offer. They gravitate to you because you have a natural ability to see the way forward and face adversity with resilience and resolve.

Maybe this natural magnetism is the result of your experience. Perhaps you have a heightened sense of empathy that allows you to connect with others in meaningful ways. After all, you are an amazing listener. Or it could be that you are simply one of the lucky few with inborn glass-half-full positivity and a possibility-oriented nature that naturally inspires people to greater heights.

Whatever the source, you are no stranger to helping others. It's who you are: a changemaker.

As a changemaker, you have likely transformed your life or significant parts of it. Through this process, you've overcome one or more seemingly "impossible" obstacles. In fact, I bet I've caught you mid-process even as we speak, currently seeking to improve your work and life in some fashion. (Admittedly, I'm cheating a little here. The simple fact that you're reading this book confirms your commitment to building a better future!)

Your gifts are unique

Your gifts place you within an elite group of individuals. Believe it or not, the ability to create and thrive in a life of your choosing, despite what comes your way, is not common.

Most people are not gifted with the skills and insight necessary to help others be at their very best, let alone successfully navigate life's most unexpected and devastating surprises. Even fewer have developed themselves through books, online courses, professional trainings, certifications, and workshops to the extent you have. You are a lifelong learner, someone who's devoted to being your best, personally and professionally. Rare is the ability to recognize the true value of life experience and professional expertise, combined with a mind focused on helping others.

Others have noticed your gifts too. If you are like many who pursue a career in coaching, it's highly likely those who know you through personal or professional relationships have said, "You should become a coach." My consulting clients were the first to recognize my coaching potential. These people, whether they be close friends, casual acquaintances or complete strangers, see the true value you innately possess. And they are right.

Who becomes a coach?

You are in good company. As someone interested in becoming a coach, you're prepared to join the tens of thousands of individuals originating from one hundred thirty-seven countries throughout the world, and almost every industry imaginable. Each brings her or his greatest gifts to a rapidly growing marketplace, employing their unique talents to serve an ideal client base.

Many choose to start their own businesses, combining their experience and expertise into a specialty niche. Others incorporate the tools and methodology of coaching into an existing role or business. At Coach Training World, we've certified people from a wide range of academic, professional, ethnic, and social backgrounds, ranging in age from eighteen to seventy-eight. These backgrounds include (but are not limited to):

- Astrologers
- Dentists
- Authors
- Attorneys
- Project Managers
- Psychologists
- Healers
- Entrepreneurs
- Marketing Specialists
- IT Professionals
- Machinists
- Parents
- Social Workers
- Graphic Artists
- College/Grad Students
- Retirees
- Hair Dressers
- HR Professionals
- Energy Workers
- Organizational Consultants
- Teachers
- Business Leaders
- Interior Designers
- Sales Professionals
- Fitness Professionals
- Speakers
- Yogis
- Nutritionists
- Counselors/ Therapists
- Metaphysical Practitioners
- Police Officers
- Physical Therapists
- Massage Therapists
- Performing Artists
- Coaches without Certification
- ...and now YOU!

No matter where you're coming from or what area you'll eventually focus on, you share the same love of helping others on a deep, meaningful, and transformative level with these other changemakers.

But before we continue forth, know this: no one is exactly like you. You are an original. You've traveled a unique road throughout your life, with experiences, knowledge and skills that are singular to you.

When you combine your life experience and unique brilliance with professional coaching, the end result is an inimitable change-making process. Only you can offer it. And your potential within your own one-of-a-kind coaching business is limited only by the goals and restrictions you set.

Your personality plays a significant factor here too. Who you are as an individual and how your clients feel around you is essential to your capacity to evoke change. In the same way you are drawn to like-minded individuals, your ideal clients admire, trust and respect who you are. They are drawn to you not only for your experience and expertise, but for your values and the perspectives you hold. For this reason, you are ideally positioned to offer guidance others can't, simply because of who you are. That originality represents tremendous value to your ideal audience, even when you offer services comparable to other coaches.

To that, I need to add one small disclaimer: you can only reach your highest potential by bringing your whole self to the world. We'll get into this in depth in the chapters that follow. But for now, I'd like you to simply be aware that the union of your whole self is what enables you to achieve your most meaningful goals and shine at your brightest. This perfect balance is also what resonates with those who need you most.

Change is a driving force

The journey to become a professional coach is personal. For some, coaching is a natural extension of their services. It complements an existing business or career enhancement. For others, like Tara (who you'll meet in just a moment), it's the beginning of a new life chapter.

After the tragic and sudden loss of her husband, Woody, Tara suddenly found herself in a place where she had no other choice but to reinvent her life. Throughout her marriage, all her plans had involved Woody. Then suddenly, their dreams of buying a house, starting a family, and traveling the world were no longer a reality. In a very short period, Tara went from the security of a happy home to an all-consuming uncertainty. Where she had once been able to see years in advance, she was now unsure of what tomorrow held. Her life partner, living situation, lifestyle, and financial stability had all been pulled out from underneath her.

Adrift in the pain and confusion of her loss, Tara started asking the bigger questions:

- Now what?
- Who am I without him and our life together?
- Who do I really want to be?
- What's my calling?

Equipped with twenty years of experience in social work, Tara knew the grieving process was going to take time. Leaning into her spirituality gave her the strength and faith she needed during this period. Yet her direction remained elusive. What she didn't know was that she was also grieving for the loss of herself and her creativity.

> *"I knew that I loved working with people and the supporting and empowering part of my old job, but I hated the exclusion of things like the deeper conversations, spirituality, and personal awareness,"* Tara reflects. *"I struggled with just wanting to go back to what I knew, the thought being: Enough changes, I just need some stability."*

In his dying days, her husband told her how much he regretted not following his passion. This regret, amplified by how quickly his life was swept away from him, served as a profound motivator for Tara. In honor of Woody, Tara decided to commit herself to a life well-lived. Her first step in her life reinvention process: to pursue meaningful work.

She began her search online, exploring various helping professions and programs that offered a holistic approach. Over the years, she had witnessed countless people, including herself, trying to make positive changes in their lives yet unable to maintain forward momentum. As an astute observer, the importance of working with the whole person was clear to Tara. It was also obvious that she wanted to serve a new population in her new career.

> *"The further I moved through [my] grief, the clearer things became,"* Tara says. *"I wanted to work with people who were ready, willing, and able to make sustainable changes in their lives – [people who] wanted to understand themselves at a deeper level. I also wanted that for myself. I just didn't totally realize it then."*

That wasn't all. Tara was also looking for work that would provide freedom. Freedom to work from anywhere, freedom to discover new things and do the things she already enjoyed, freedom to spend time with her friends and family. In the end, professional coaching ended up being a natural fit.

> "[I] was brought to tears with the explanation of coaching. It checks all of the boxes," Tara says with a smile.

Today you'll find Tara running two businesses with her canine sidekick, Bramble. Through her coaching business, she champions others to create their own transition after a disastrous life event. Offering her Plan B programs and personal coaching services, Tara successfully integrates her vast experience in social work with her own experience processing the loss of her husband.

Tara now works with middle-aged women who have gone through one of the "5 Ds": death, divorce, dumped, downsized, or disease. These women have had their lives shaken to the core and are on the other side of the grieving process, ready to reinvent. Like Tara, they've come to a place where they're starting to question what's next, reevaluate where their lives are going, and revisit their life plans. With Tara's support, these women rediscover what it is they truly want, realizing that – although traumatic – their particular "D" actually represents a new starting point.

In addition to her private client work, Tara provides much-needed support for social workers. She champions them to refocus their attention on their own self-care while simultaneously helping others.

Becoming a coach also helped Tara listen to her own desires and improve her life in all areas. Through travel, exploration, and photography, Tara has addressed her need for creative expression that she had inadvertently left behind when life got busy.

"I now have freedom to coach from anywhere as long as I have a computer. Being my own boss allows me to set my own schedule. This enables me to have an awesome, grounding morning routine that gets my day off to a great start," she says.

Tara was faced with a transition – a type of change that none of us choose yet all of us confront at least once in our lives. Despite the shock, grief and upending of the life she had known until then, Tara discovered a valuable lesson. Adversity offers us a rare opportunity to examine our feelings and desires. It also helps us return to the core of who we are. With time and the right kind of support, we can reinvent our lives for the better.

Even though we may not have volunteered for them, life-changes often provide a tremendous gift: the blank page and the capacity to write a new story.

Christine offers a similar example. After a difficult divorce and fighting hard for the future of her kids, Christine came to Whole Person Coaching wanting to start her own business. With advanced degrees and studies in communication — including non-violent communication and conflict mediation, among other disciplines — she was no stranger to looking at the depths of human nature. Like many of our coaches, Christine had acquired numerous qualifications and certifications as a devotee in the personal growth arena. Add to that her hard-earned experience in working through the most difficult relationship of her life, and it was plain to see: Christine had traveled the road firsthand.

She was on a mission, one that was near and dear to her heart. Christine wanted to change the way divorce affected the family, especially kids. She believed that, despite divorce, peaceful parenting could be possible.

Like so many members of the Coach Training World coaching community, Christine listened to her inner calling to do greater work in the world – work that would provide the lifestyle and community she deeply valued. Today she works with a wide variety of clients, helping them create happier outcomes from difficult divorces.

Bring your whole self to your work

Many of us find ourselves with less and less time and an unmanageable increase in obligations. On top of that, there are numerous expectations we place on ourselves. It's no wonder an overwhelming segment of the population remains discontent and trapped in jobs, relationships and other situations that limit who they can be and what is possible in their lives.

Derek was a perfect example. He had a severe case of corporate burnout. But he decided to go against the odds and reclaim those lost aspects of his persona by aligning with his entrepreneurial spirit.

From the tender age of fifteen, Derek knew there was more to life. Yet out of loyalty and obligation to his parents (who had worked countless hours to keep food on the table for him and his two siblings), he adhered to their wishes. He pursued a practical degree in college and got a "good" corporate job. There he stalled. Twenty-one years passed before he finally woke up and broke free.

After engaging in conversations with various change-making entrepreneurs, Derek flashed forward into his current career. What he saw left him filled with fear and regret. He felt empty. His future appeared meaningless and full of things that didn't truly matter. A few months later, he resigned from his corporate job to start his journey into coaching and entrepreneurship.

Derek's first step was to work with a coach. In doing so, he came to understand the power of partnering with someone who can help you figure it out for yourself. Before long, his future as a guide and supporter of others began to take shape. He chose to become a professional coach and support others in their efforts to escape the nine-to-five existence.

Today, Derek thrives within a group of people exactly like him—men and women who instinctively know or come to realize a vital truth: their career path isn't their calling. He helps them identify and break the chains of the outdated stories and expectations that hold them back from the success and life enjoyment they truly desire. Already the go-to champion for friends, family, and coworkers, Derek recognized the opportunity to extend his knowledge and skills to a broader audience.

Derek's success was not overnight. He took some big risks and worked hard to make sure they weren't for naught. Ironically, he points to his tenure in corporate America as part of the foundation of his success as a coach. By taking the things that worked and discarding those that didn't, he was able to build on his existing experience, and on his own terms, using his corporate experience as a calling card.

Stop for a moment and think about all the ways you could do the very same thing. Think you have nothing to share? Many of us started out questioning our value. Yet without knowing you personally, I guarantee your experience has more value than you know. We'll begin to discover it together as we get into the journal exercises later in this chapter and those that follow. But for now, simply know that – like Derek – you don't have to follow a pre-ordained path.

You and only you should determine the course of your life.

Deepen the impact of your existing business

Derek is not alone in his desire for happiness, freedom and prosperity. Who among us doesn't want that? For this reason, people around the globe are now turning to coaching and Whole Person Coaching in particular. It is one of the few methods of personal and professional development focused on working deeply with the whole person toward human excellence and life mastery.

Whole Person Coaching's holistic tools and techniques enable people to shift from their head (and the confinements of "rational" adult behavior, or the expectations of others) into the desires embedded within their hearts and souls. More significantly, it also allows people to leverage their very best to create meaningful, rewarding careers and lives.

One common application is the pairing of coaching skills with another specialty. You'll notice this more and more within service-oriented businesses. The reason is simple yet powerful: coaching shifts the conversation from a one-sided list of things someone has to do to an empowering relationship that cultivates deep motivation in others. This approach elicits a noticeably greater degree of buy-in among clients by focusing on their individual goals, while addressing any road blocks or limiting beliefs.

Kelly and Martin McFarland are a perfect example. They're a husband and wife team who successfully leveraged the power of coaching to dramatically improve their own lives, as well as the lives of their clients.

As a Whole Person Certified Coach and Posture Alignment Therapist, Kelly uses the tools and techniques of coaching to rapidly invite change, shift perspectives, and ignite new behaviors in her clients. It's worth noting that some of these individuals endure substantial physical pain with varying levels of disability. Through her coach training, Kelly is able to address the numerous emotional and mental factors related to her client's discomfort and restrictive lifestyle, offering an enhanced level of service that further sets her apart from her competition.

Kelly's journey into coaching began while she was working at the Egoscue corporate office in San Diego. After joining a networking group, Kelly met a coach she describes as "dynamic and amazing." They decided to trade services, and Kelly instantly found herself turning around the tools, language and processes she picked up from her own coaching experience and repurposing them for use with her own clients.

> *"It's funny because the whole time I was working at the corporate office, I kept thinking 'Gosh, there's this disconnect between the technical side of what I was needing to do with my clients, in a therapeutic sense, and the communication that needed to happen to connect with them and get them to that deeper level of trust,'" Kelly says, "a level that would help them sustain change in their lives."*

During her own coaching sessions, Kelly created a strategic life plan, detailing in reverse where she wanted to be in five years, three years, one year, six months, and three months. Her goals included everything from cultivating a great relationship that would transition into marriage to becoming the owner of a franchised business. Today, she and her husband Martin co-own the Egoscue clinic in Portland, Oregon.

Inspired by the coaching process, Kelly and Martin decided to become professional coaches and integrate these powerful skills into their clinic. Shortly after the completion of their training, they began to leverage a complementary mix of coaching, education, and empowerment into the individual Egoscue exercise programs. Whole Person Coaching's highly customizable nature provided the perfect match to a form of physical therapy that is, in itself, also highly personal and transformative.

> *"Coaching is ninety-nine percent of what I do," Kelly says. "I do so much interpersonal work with people! I would not be where I am today—both in my personal life and from a financial/business standpoint—without those tools."*

As for Martin, Whole Person Coaching's focus on listening to hear (as opposed to the more customary practice of listening to respond) transformed the way he works with clients.

Integrating Whole Person Coaching techniques into his work, Martin shifted his line of questioning. Where he previously may have asked something like, "Is this painful?" he now uses open-ended and neutral questions like, "What sensations are you experiencing?" and "What might this information mean to you?"

"We invite them to tune into their whole being and listen to the early warning signs that their bodies are communicating," Martin says. "We move the focus toward what's happening in the present moment versus what could be in the future. As individuals, we pay so much attention to the end goal, we miss the journey. Change happens in the present. Starting at the zero point, clearing your mind of negative energy, and connecting to your whole self and your life in positive ways, things can flow if you trust and accept them."

So far, we've seen how Tara, Christine, Derek, Kelly and Martin improved their lives and individual services through coach training. But this book is about you making your impact in the world. Here's what you can expect in the weeks and months that will follow should you pursue this life-enhancing pathway.

Your future self will thank you

It's impossible to elaborate on the countless ways coaching can improve and change all aspects of your life for the better. But I would like to share five of the biggest benefits you'll receive as a professionally trained coach.

Benefit #1: Becoming a professional coach allows you to transfer all your skills, experience, training and expertise into a new career and business.

No matter how great or small, your experience and expertise, coupled with the coaching process, can be applied to someone's personal or professional life. In fact, many people come into coaching certain they want to help others without knowing exactly how they'll make it happen. Through the training process, they become radically clear on their gifts, talents, passions, and purpose. From there, they build their next career and business around who they are at their best.

Believe it or not, you have a lot more to share with others than you think. And the beauty of coaching is that everything you've gained throughout your life is applicable.

Benefit #2: Becoming a professional coach empowers you to pursue work that is meaningful and enjoyable.

You love helping others. What better way to do so than to light the way and inspire people to be all of who they are and to pursue and accomplish their greatest dreams?

Coaching is designed around the client. But it's also for you. One of the many benefits of coach training is that you receive coaching in the process, instilling similar benefits throughout the many aspects of your life. In fact, you can rediscover the whole of who you are while manifesting your best possible life and career.

The benefits of coaching also increase exponentially as you coach others. That's because of the unique collaborative process and empowering relationship you experience with your clients. The coaching relationship brings out the best in you and your client by operating inside a courageous space. In such an environment, you both grow, learn, and evolve together inside the process.

Plus, another bonus: it's extremely likely your clients will also inspire and motivate you to pursue things you hadn't even considered.

Benefit #3: Becoming a professional coach ensures your business works for you, not the other way around.

By becoming a coach, you create a life and business on your terms. This is realized not only through a preferable schedule, but also by where, how and with whom you work. Want to work from home? Travel abroad? No problem. You can work from anywhere in the world.

Imagine you're on vacation with the kids (or dogs, if you're like me) and your phone dings an alert. You swipe the screen to unlock and see someone has just purchased one of your products. Not only are you thrilled with the income while making a difference in someone else's life, but your vacation has also just been paid for!

You can further extend your impact, influence and income potential as you gain clarity around your ideal clients, their needs, and the kinds of changes you'd like to create. Examples include coaching programs, products, and an array of passive income streams.

Benefit #4: Becoming a professional coach offers a rare opportunity to find inner peace, tranquility and work-life balance.

As a professional Whole Person Coach, you are essentially an agent of change. At the core, you are devoted to creating balance, harmony, vitality, and happiness for yourself and others. Imagine what it would be like to wake up in the morning without the instant bombardment of the pressures, fearful anticipation and negativity that are often part of working for others. One of my biggest lessons over the years is that, in the business of change, we are actively modeling self-care. Creating and sustaining work-life balance is part of the job. Gone are the days of work till you drop. And good riddance!

Benefit #5: Becoming a professional coach isn't just about your clients.

Many students have informed me that the training alone is worth their investment just for the tools and techniques they gain. They consistently report that the holistic approach they learned enabled them to change their own life, and also made it possible to change their relationships – all for the better.

Learning how to listen and respond inside difficult conversations and how to show up with confidence, authentically expressing yourself, brings you closer to spouses, partners, friends, family, and coworkers. That's because the language of coaching is intentionally designed to create trust, connection and unconditional support with others.

But it doesn't stop there. As a coach trainee, you'll have ample opportunity to use the tools and processes firsthand, and receive the support to make your own life enhancements. In coaching, everybody wins.

I could keep going, but let's get back to you and why you're here.

What brought you here?

Each of us has our own reasons for wanting to become a coach. Some of us are tired of the daily grind, working for a boss or company that continuously fails to recognize our value. Others choose coaching because someone else noticed their unique capacity for listening, offering perspective, and championing change in others. Some people simply have a natural tank of energy to burn and want something that truly challenges them. And we all love the engagement and new experiences that come from helping others.

Like those who traveled the road to become a professional coach, you too can pursue meaningful work and create a life you'll absolutely love. You too can bring your whole self to life!

Regardless of where you are in your own life, you can choose the roads you'll travel. You too can be who you truly are. The commitment you make to yourself and your future will be well rewarded. That's because, as a professional coach, you can create a life you'll absolutely love – being who you are at your best – and pioneer the business that will make it all possible.

Chapter review and coming attractions

In this chapter, we explored how coaching has changed the lives of people just like you. The examples we looked at exemplify coaching's unique combination of life experience and individual brilliance in the pursuit of work that is meaningful and enjoyable. This is how you create services only you can offer. Remember, you are ideally positioned to offer guidance others can't simply because of who you are. By transferring your existing skills, experience, training and expertise into a new career and business, you offer tremendous value to your ideal audience. And suddenly, you're in a business that works for you, not the other way around.

Next up: We'll explore the one thing that keeps most people's greatest potential hidden from view, and their greatest gifts from being fully expressed. Learn what you'll need to overcome to effectively serve those who need you most and become the successful coach you are meant to be.

~ *In Your Journal* ~

As I mentioned in the Introduction, I'm giving you contemplative exercises to explore your unique situation and start developing the skills you'll need as a Whole Person coach.

I recommend taking the time to write out your responses in a physical journal or computer document. You'll be amazed at the depth and clarity you'll experience through the act of getting your thoughts and feelings out of your head and onto paper.

In fact, the insight you gain will be essential as you move forward through the book. It will serve as the foundation for your personal rediscovery and learning process, providing the focus, direction, and clarity you seek to create your own preferred future as a professional coach.

So let's start by laying the groundwork...

- Describe how you first felt when you discovered coaching was a real profession, one in which you could earn a healthy living by helping others. What excited you the most?

- What difference would you like to make in the world? How are you already enhancing the lives of others? After listing your current efforts, include additional ways you would like to help others, and any differences (big and small) you'd like to make in the world.

- And finally, list the things in your own life that becoming a professional coach would enable you to do. Don't think small — you can truly have it all. A life, career and business you truly love.

~2~

Your Life-Changing Career Awaits

Answer the call

Coaching is all about championing others toward their best while they navigate exciting or challenging transitions in their lives. That change begins with you. There has never been a better time to become a professional coach.

As a young child, I remember a magical conversation with my grandma. She was in the back bedroom one sunny autumn afternoon quietly making beds. As I walked into the room, she took my hand and walked me over to a large cedar chest. It was covered with faded wool blankets, their edges slightly frayed from years of providing warmth during our cold Portland, Oregon winters.

My grandma removed an ornate key from a little drawer in her nightstand and gently unlocked the chest. As I peered inside, she explained, "This is a hope chest. Someday it will be yours. It's a secret place to hold your treasures – your keepsakes – what you cherish most for a future day. I keep my most precious things in here."

Giddy about having a treasure chest, I asked, "Can anything go in here?"

"Of course," my grandmother replied with joy as she closed and locked the chest. "Anything and everything that is most meaningful to you."

What have you set aside for the future?

If you are like most of us, you've buried away some of your most precious assets within an internal treasure chest: your personality, passions, gifts and talents. For a myriad of reasons, it wasn't the right situation or moment to let those parts of you shine. Maybe you pursued a practical college degree because it made sense (and others agreed). Or you endured that particular boss for years – the one who failed to see your potential – because you needed the money.

I recall a very unfortunate man, we'll call Phillip, who had spent most of his life dredging away at a job that left him feeling lifeless and exhausted. He sat, watching others – including his own children – take the risks necessary to jump into more meaningful careers and lives. But much like his own father, he held on to the status quo until the bitter end.

During his last five years of employment, at the age of 62, Philip began to plan his ideal life after retirement. An animal lover, Phillip had dreams of inventing his own holistic pet care product. His goal was to improve an animal's health and extend its longevity through tailored herbal recommendations for type, size and breed. In his spare time, he planned to travel the world and finally spend long-missed quality time with his family. But two months after retirement, Phillip died of a heart attack.

It's a tragic story. But what makes it even sadder is how common and universal it is.

Change calls to us in many forms

Reading this book, you might already recognize your own "calling" for what it is. Or perhaps like many others, it became obvious as you were exposed to something entirely new, whether it be ideas, people, opportunities or environments. Regardless of the source of your awakening, you are now aware of a deeper calling within. You are suddenly attuned to the fulfillment and joy life can bestow upon you once you tap into your own passions and potential effectively. You know the importance of stepping into a bigger and more fully-expressed version of yourself in service to others.

But will you?

The great divide

In his book *The War of Art*, Steven Pressfield wrote, "Most of us have two lives. The life we live, and the unlived life within us. Between the two stands Resistance."[1] It is the all-too-common practice of yielding to Resistance, Pressfield observed, that "deforms our spirit. It stunts us and makes us less than we are and were born to be."

Resistance, as Pressfield termed it, presents itself in a variety of forms. Most common among them is fear. It attacks us through a host of different forces, many of which we are raised to trust and defer to. They range from friends, family, teachers and coworkers to societal pressures delivered through media representations and advertising. Even (and often most notoriously) our own mind provides the negative self-talk that keeps us locked in fearful struggle for years.

Sadly, the practice of relenting to the toxic, undermining forces of fear, doubt and the great divide they create between the life we live and the one we truly want is not limited to one group of individuals. Despite socioeconomic standing, national origin, race, gender, creed, and sexual orientation, we all deal with many of the same stumbling blocks throughout our lives.

Even the best of us hit the proverbial snooze button and refuse to heed the call. Instead, we drudge our way through a job, a relationship, or a life that is unfulfilling and even potentially hazardous to our well-being.

Change and fear go hand in hand

As a changemaker, you already know how the effects of fear can paralyze people – despite the fact they have everything they need to move ahead in their lives. Fear

---

1 Pressfield, Steven. 2002. *The War of Art*. New York: Black Irish Entertainment LLC.

becomes so deep-seeded, many people never even recognize they are under its influence.

A recent paper entitled "Emotion and Decision Making," submitted for publication in the *Annual Review of Psychology*, reported that:

> *"Fear involves low certainty and a low sense of control, which are likely to produce a perception of negative events as unpredictable and situationally determined."*[2]

Who doesn't take a step back from their dreams and desires when making such changes would mean venturing into new territories and an unpredictable future? Simple things such as lack of know-how and information quickly translate into anticipatory thinking that produces worst-case scenarios. Often told to us by that voice in our mind referred to as the "inner protector" or "inner critic," these stories frequently undermine our ability to see our potential and the possibility of a better future. In such ways, fear prevents those who are under its influence from enjoying the richness and life-fulfillment that would otherwise be readily available to them.

Conducted by researchers from Harvard, University of California, Irvine, Claremont McKenna College, and Carnegie Mellon, the aforementioned study was particularly insightful for its conclusions:

> *"Although emotions may influence decisions through multiple mechanisms, considerable evidence reveals that effects occur via changes in (a) content of thought,*

2 Lerner, Jennifer S., Ye Li, Piercarlo Valdesolo, and Karim S. Kassam. 2015. "Emotion and Decision Making." *Annual Review of Psychology* 66 (1): 799-823.

(b) depth of thought, and (c) content of implicit goals..."

This speaks to the importance of being mindful on where we place our attention and the lens we choose to view ourselves, others and the world we live in. Let's not forget the unconscious factors that undermine our success. Your life is as you envision it, and can be as you design it.

Don't let fear hold you back!

Fear is an unpleasant emotional response. It's a psychobiological status report sent out by the most primitive part of your brain (the amygdala) in an effort to keep you safe. Taking cues from your sensory organs, it is triggered when your amygdala interprets information to mean that someone or something is dangerous, likely to cause pain, or threaten your safety, situation or those you care about. Fear is an innate response intended to ensure your survival. It dates back to the earliest days of our species when we were under constant threat of mortal danger by larger, more powerful predators.

In today's modern world, fear and the way in which it expresses itself in your thoughts, feelings, behaviors and interactions with others, can have a very real impact on your ability to achieve your goals and dreams. What about right now? As you think about starting a new career or business, one that may even feel like an impossible dream? What arises?

If you are like many in the midst of a significant transition, you might recognize the effects of fear as the narrator in your mind. The voice that reminds you of the risks of venturing into a new career. The one that beckons you back to the status quo. A voice you are likely familiar with from other moments in time where you were about to step into new territory.

Once you move past fear and into your new life-changing career (and the life it brings you), you are forever changed for the better. Because the process is that much easier the next time around. Your fears will fade.

The same will be true for your clients. In fact, fear is often what brings a client to your doorstep, though they themselves may not even be aware of it initially. It's what prevents them from being who they are, and having the life they were meant to live.

Simplified? Yes.

You and I both know it takes more than logic to overcome fear. But it can be overcome. In fact, that's exactly what you learn when training to become a Whole Person Coach. As you become aware of and understand the intricate nature of fear and an individual's inner landscape, the mystery becomes quite solvable – both for you and for your clients.

Many graduates have shared with me that one of the central reasons they trained to become a coach was to obtain the capacity to face their fears and abolish their self-doubt. (Addressing fear and doubt is primary to the work of a Whole Person Coach!) The other reason almost universally shared is the acquisition of clarity, a good map and an accurate compass. For how can you expect to effectively face fear without knowing what's ahead?

Ironically, we already have our compass – it's the intersection of our deepest passions, purpose and potential. The trick is to reclaim those lost aspects of your personality and potential and to learn to access and trust the wisdom that lives within. Doing so allows you to align with your true calling and bring your best self into the world.

The world needs you now

As a changemaker, you don't need the intercession of a life-altering event or an existence that simply plays out someone else's dreams — like the examples we saw in Chapter 1 — to realize the cost of an unlived life. People regret missed opportunities and the freedoms they sacrificed to meet the expectations and needs of others. They regret the neglected relationships that were important, especially when they've ended up lonely, angry, discontent, and directionless, without a tribe of their own. Above all: people regret their failure to pursue the things that truly mattered to them by not taking the risks to strive for something better.

This is why the world needs you. No one deserves to miss out on life's opportunities and potential. No one should live a life that is anything less than fulfilling. No one should remain invisible or cloaked and unable to express their true authentic self. And no one should have to face the end regretting the path not taken. That includes you above all!

The shift toward this best possible future begins with you. And it begins now.

As a coach, you offer your clients thought-provoking conversations that light the way to fresh perspectives and novel approaches. As someone who has already been providing a similar type of support informally, you'll be thankful to learn that never have more people been hiring coaches, attending workshops, and purchasing online coaching programs than right now. There has also been a substantial rise in the quantity and variety of coaches hired by corporations and coaching firms in today's market. And the numbers only continue to increase.

Before we move on, take a moment to consider the following statistics from the *2016 ICF Global Coaching Study:*[3]

- **7.6 billion:** number of potential clients in the world (yes, that's the global population… and why not?)

- **53,300:** number of professionally trained coaches currently offering services globally

- **$2.4 billion:** annual revenue generated by these coaching services

- **Latin America and the Caribbean:** two of the fastest growing markets for coaching products and services

- **3 out of 4:** coaches who operate in North America, western Europe, and Oceania

- **1:** the number of people who can offer the unique combination of experience, expertise and passion you can

Once considered a luxury service designed for CEOs and celebrities, coaching is now a mainstream, credible and respected career path used by millions of people pursuing a happier, healthier and more productive life. Promoted in print, on TV, and throughout the web, the

---

3 International Coach Federation. *2016 ICF Global Coaching Study.* Research. Accessed April 4, 2018. https://coachfederation.org/research/global-coaching-study.

science and application of coaching make it the number one, fastest growing change-making method in the world. And the reason is simple: there are people in the world right now who need your wisdom.

It's a journey with a highly desirable destination

You have everything you need to become a successful coach if you are willing to learn and commit yourself to what it takes. The remainder of this book is devoted to exploring the roadmap you'll need to become a successful coach and thrive in a life and business you love. But this isn't just any roadmap. It's tailor-made for who you are and where you want to go. It is based on the four core attributes of successful coaches who have paved the way before you. Coaches who stand out and prosper within a crowded marketplace, being who they are at their best.

The four core attributes we will explore are:

1. Holistic coaching skills & change process knowledge

2. Credibility & legitimacy

3. Personal mastery

4. Business, marketing & sales skills

Some of these may seem obvious. But here's a hard truth: few coaches commit themselves to these best practices. As you might also guess, they unwittingly become part of the statistics for failure simply because they don't follow the right footsteps.

Holistic coaching skills & change process knowledge

Let's start with the obvious: you are good with people. You're an amazing listener and others depend on you for your perspective and advice. Helping others comes naturally to you. It's why you're here. As someone others depend on for advice and perspective, you know the benefits of firsthand life experience and expertise to lean on. But it takes more than experience and information alone to evoke sustainable change in others.

Training to become a professional coach ensures you have a comprehensive understanding of the science and psychology that inform and guide you in your change-making processes. You also develop the skills required to help your clients overcome the fears, self-limiting stories and sabotaging habits that prevent them from having what they truly deserve.

An important aspect in your development as a coach is your ability to work with what arises during the coaching relationship. If you are good with people, it's guaranteed your clients will bring their whole self – mind, body, heart and spirit – to the conversation. This means your coaching skills and toolkit should go beyond using intellect and reasoning as your process. As someone who understands and includes your client's emotional, social, somatic and spiritual influences in your coaching approach, you address the real underlying issues and the client's greatest needs.

Being able to assist your clients to navigate both their inner and outer worlds and draw upon the multiple intelligences within is what differentiates you from other coaches. It's also what elevates you from a "transactional" coach, one who merely helps clients establish and accomplish goals, to someone who truly transforms lives in more ways than one.

With all this in mind, it is vital to develop and deepen your capacity to consistently and sustainably evoke positive change in others. Your reputation is one of your greatest assets. Remember: no results, no repeat business. No raving reviews, no referrals.

We'll continue this conversation inside Chapters 3 and 4. You'll learn why changemakers across the world rely on Whole Person Coaching to affect change on personal and professional levels, and a global scale.

Personal mastery

Training to become a coach should be about you as the instrument of change. After all, you are the common denominator in all of the work you do. Developing your capacity to be highly effective in helping others goes beyond learning basic coaching skills. You're now delving into the realm of personal mastery.

That's why you'll quickly notice that the Whole Person Coaching method is designed to immerse you into the change-making process as a key element. Anyone can offer their clients coaching tools and processes to follow. Who you are and how you work with others is your secret weapon to success. The more you work on your own communication, relationship-building skills and presence, the more effective you'll be with others. Guaranteed.

And the payback is practically instantaneous. The way you engage and interact with your clients contributes to the creative, collaborative partnership you forge with them.

As a whole person, you too have many aspects to your personality and the way you view and navigate the world. Working on yourself increases your self-awareness and self-understanding. This insight enables you to recognize ways in which you impact the coaching process. It also reveals how you can amplify your capacity to bring greater value to your work and clients.

For most coaches, this news is well-embraced. Many have discovered this aspect of training to add considerable value not just to their training but to their lives overall. And who among us doesn't love improving our personal communications and deepening our relationships? As a bonus, the training serves as a free license to focus on you "mastering you." Deeply knowing and embracing your whole self allows you to shine at your best in service to others.

Business, marketing & sales skills

Excuse me as I rant a bit here, but nothing breaks my heart more than an amazing coach who remains undiscovered. Not only do clients who need them suffer, the coaches themselves often give up on their own true value and settle for work that's nothing more than a paycheck. While we all must make a living, our lives can be so much more than work-for-pay.

To prosper in the business of change, you must be willing to learn, grow and develop your business as much as you are willing to help others. And there is no better way to do this than to get the help you need from someone who has successfully traveled the road before you.

One of the biggest mistakes new and prospective coaches make is to invest in coach training then settle for a do-it-yourself approach to starting their business. Launching and succeeding in your business requires specific business skills, an empowered mindset, and expert mentoring. You'll also need guidance navigating what will feel like endless decisions, especially if you hope to avoid costly mistakes.

While I can't possibly cover every detail in this book, I've devoted Chapter 5 to helping you create your own one-of-a-kind niche, one that combines your best in service to those you love most. In Chapter 6, you'll learn about the Spiral Growth Coaching Business Model. This is where you'll discover the secrets to growing and sustaining a coaching business, and explore the different niches available to you.

Credibility & legitimacy

With the proliferation of the coaching profession, your number one priority is to distinguish yourself from others. You might hear this as "define your niche," which is one essential ingredient to success. But it's far from the only one.

Earning your ICF credential positions you above ninety-five percent of coaches working today. It demonstrates your commitment to coaching excellence and aligns you with an organization known for credibility and results the world over. As an ICF-credentialed coach, you are indeed a legitimate, professionally-trained changemaker, recognized and respected by companies and individuals alike. Much like a doctor, accountant, beautician or therapist who goes through a credentialing process, your future clients and employers know they're hiring a trained coach who meets standardized requirements.

In today's marketplace, more and more employers and individual coaching clients are vetting a coach's credentials through the ICF (which we'll talk more about in Chapter 7).

Chapter review and coming attractions

This is a lot to think about. But all those who have succeeded as professional coaches know that meaningful change doesn't happen overnight. You've put yourself on this path for a reason. Trust that decision. Trust yourself! I can't promise the results will be immediate, but they will be exponential.

By training as a professional coach, you become part of a community of supportive people on a similar journey, developing their coaching skills and starting their businesses right alongside you. This type of involvement also keeps you committed and connected to the dream-career and life you truly deserve. Through this journey, you uncover more about yourself than you ever thought possible. You discover who you are at the core and what matters most to you.

Coaching is not just a living, it's a life. Training to become a coach provides more than just the opportunity to step into a meaningful career or business. It allows you to selectively create your dream come true world from top to bottom.

Next Up: We'll continue learning what it takes to become a successful coach. I'll share the specifics of our proprietary coaching modality, Whole Person Coaching. You'll learn the core tools that amplify what you're capable of achieving, and why global changemakers choose it over every other type of coach training available! (Hint: it has to do with results.)

~ In Your Journal ~

- How you are feeling right now about creating change in your life?

- Imagine your preferred future as a professional coach in a dream job or business you love. Describe your perfect day. How will you spend your time?

- Next, create a list of action steps that could lead you into this new direction, as well as the things you'll need to act (whether it's emotional support or financial resources).

- Imagine for a moment you've made all your desired changes with this preferred future in mind? How are you feeling now?

~3~

Whole Person Coaching: Tools for change

When an individual comes to know, embrace and express all aspects of their wholeness, they are positioned to thrive in any aspect of life. They become rich in resources, grounded in their being, and at peace within.

Times are indeed a changin'. In the swift-paced, dynamic and often chaotic world we live in, coaches are now called upon to contribute their best in deeper, and more meaningful ways than ever before. This shift represents quite a journey from where we all started. In its infancy, coaching was found only in C-level suites and among celebrities seeking to play their highest game. But the tools and methodology of professional coaching are now applied to just about every personal and professional niche – a list that grows continually as the profession and its applications advance. This trend positions coaches in unlimited markets throughout the world. More importantly, it enriches your work as a coach.

It's a tremendously exciting time to be a coach. Especially for those of us who enjoy the intricacies that accompany personal growth and professional development. The role you'll play in your client's life and the changes you'll support them to achieve are limited only by your imagination.

Meeting the needs and demands of today's diverse client base, Whole Person Coaching advances the standard tools and techniques of our profession to produce noticeably higher levels of success. The difference is Whole Person Coaching draws upon and integrates every aspect of an individual into the process – mind, body, heart and spirit. It brings out their very best while sustainably addressing that which holds them back. This is what makes it so effective. It truly works with the whole person, inside and out, giving you the inner edge to produce the results other methodologies simply cannot.

Whole Person Coaching methodology

The effectiveness of Whole Person Coaching stems from the interrelated nature that exists between the coaching relationship, communication and process. It is enhanced greatly by the coach's own work toward personal and professional mastery.

The efficacy of Whole Person Coaching stems from four key components:

1. **Revolutionary relationship** you co-create with your clients

2. **Catalytic Communication** you employ to generate self-awareness, learning and positive momentum

3. **Thought-provoking, holistic process** you offer your clients to deepen the impact and sustainability of their change

4. **Personal mastery** you embody as one who lights the way for others to discover their best self

In this chapter, we'll take a behind-the-scenes look at the first two components. These are the primary relational and communication skills of Whole Person Coaching. They shape the foundation that enables the transformative processes and depth of work to occur.

In the chapter to follow, we'll deepen our understanding through an exploration of multiple case studies to illustrate the process and the importance of the coach's presence and self-mastery in shaping the session outcomes.

Revolutionary relationship

The unique, empowering and authentic relationship you cultivate is an essential ingredient to the accomplishments you'll achieve with others. A "revolutionary relationship," as we call it, has the power to elicit the best from both coach and client alike.

From the moment you begin working with your client, and often upon your first introduction, you cultivate and sustain a deep connection. It's a professional, yet intimate relationship rooted in authenticity, trust and transparency. One that is further enriched by the respect and unconditional belief you hold toward your client's potential and the numerous possibilities that exist for them.

Imagine being in a relationship where you feel completely at ease with who you are. In this expectation- and judgment-free space, you are safe to fully express yourself and share your deepest dreams, brilliant ideas and intimate struggles. No matter what you share, you are heard and met unconditionally. Someone who confidently champions your success as you define it, dancing alongside you while honoring who you are and what you want most. Finally, imagine moving toward your best life, knowing you possess everything you need to succeed (personally and professionally) because of this sacred space – one that has been created just for you.

Envision the impact such an empowering partnership could have on your life. What could you accomplish if such a courageous space was made available to you?

Cultivating courageous space

You likely came into coaching because you or others noticed the ease and comfort people experience with you. Or maybe it was your innate knack for coaching those around you. But like so many professional coaches who began right where you are today, you may also have noticed a craving for more than your own personal experience and intuition to rely upon. When you train to become a coach, you become equipped with the skills, tools and expert mentoring that ensure you produce the results for others you know are possible.

The following coaching techniques are a sample of what you'll learn when you train to become a Whole Person Coach. They will play a huge role in your success as you work toward your client's best. That's because they start by doing the same for you!

Attuning: the power of presence

Attuning is an intentional act of focusing your attention on the client and the coaching process. Attuned, you are deeply present in the moment, curious and open to what is about to emerge. You possess a quiet mind, calm body and open heart. It's much like the first time you saw a newborn baby (whether it was of the human or furry variety). Or a precious moment when you felt deeply connected to a loved one, the divine source, nature or even your own true self. Your sense of wonder and curiosity are wide open, taking it all in.

When you "attune" with your clients, you:

- Stay deeply present to the client as they open, share and begin to disclose all that matters most

- Avoid thoughts unrelated to the client and the coaching process, keeping attention focused solely on the present moment

- Sustain a deep interest and curiosity in the client and the conversation, and an openness to receiving all that seeks to emerge

- Remain undistracted by temporary manifestations of failure, negativity or environmental noise

- Recognize when you've lost contact and take measures to reconnect to the conversation

- Notice when your client is elsewhere in the conversation and respond accordingly

Attuning enables you to build rapport and trust in any relationship. This makes it a critical skill applicable in many aspects of life. As a coach, the more attuned you are, the more powerful and effective your communication becomes. It puts you in sync with the client, the process and your presence as the coach. This state of deep presence also makes it possible for you to absorb the vital information and feedback you need to adapt your coaching style. From this position, your impact is practically limitless.

But like many of the skills you'll learn when you train to become a coach, attuning isn't just for coaches. As a coach, there may be times when you assist your clients to become more present as well. This can take many forms – from being more present within the coaching conversation and to their own needs and feelings, or simply more present in general as they make their way through daily life. Your goal is to invite them to become more awake and aware of their wholeness as a practice in mind, body, heart and spirit.

Believing: faith in self, others and the process

As a "believer" you maintain confidence in your client, yourself and the power of human potential. You are optimistic because you know anything is truly possible. Believing is a skill that serves coach and client alike. It deepens self-trust, strengthening the entire coaching process.

Believing propels your ability to champion the best from others. This is evidenced by the way you engage with your clients. They sense your positive regard and faith in their human capacity. As a result, they feel more confident and comfortable to face their doubt and fear. From this place of confidence, they step into their greatest potential and strengths. You may have felt a similar confidence when a loved one or close friend had your back during a difficult situation. Someone who held a light for you, who believed in your ability to find your way again.

When you "believe" in your clients, you:

- Patiently allow things to unfold in their own time and manner

- Remain optimistic, compassionate and enthusiastic

- Use positive words, phrases, intonations and gestures

- Extend faith in your client, even when their inner-critic has taken hold

- Support your client's journey of self-discovery and accomplishment by highlighting what is working

- Resist solving your client's problem and instead invite the client to do their own work

It's not always easy. But believing in others (not to mention yourself) is a mental capacity that can be developed over time. It often begins by dealing with your own disempowering self-talk. This includes that inner critic and its many versions. One of the most proactive ways to do this is to find ways to trust yourself in your own life first. For example, you might lean on your intuition, capacity and worthiness to succeed. Once you recognize your unlimited potential, it's much easier to see how others possess this capacity too. We are all capable of learning, growing and evolving into versions of our best self.

A simple practice to develop this trust is to write down a list of all your successes in life. What have you figured out in your life? What challenges have you overcome? What have you accomplished? Don't just focus on big wins. Those little daily victories count too! Did you eat an apple instead of ice cream for dessert last night? Did you eat a single serving of ice cream instead of the whole pint? Anything like this can be considered a win and deserves a place of honor on your list. Your successes are relevant no matter how small or insignificant they may seem to you. Because the things that may seem small to you could represent something nearly insurmountable to someone else.

Mirroring and backtracking

Imagine standing in front of a mirror. As you gaze at your reflection, the mirror accurately reflects what it sees. When you turn your head, your mirrored counterpart does the same. It also views your posture and facial expressions into the reflected image. Now imagine if the mirror was also a sounding board that reflected not only how you look but what you are saying and how you are saying it (tone, speed, inflections)? Your magical 'mirror on the wall' would convey more than just your reflection. It would offer a message reflective of your words – spoken and unspoken. This is the best way to describe the practice of mirroring and backtracking.

At the beginning of the coaching relationship, your goal is to develop fast rapport and trust with your client. As you reflect your client's words, key phrases and gestures, they get a felt sense that you truly see, hear and understand them. This is further reinforced by the way in which you listen and reflect their words from a place of curiosity and "not-knowing." Later in the coaching process, these forms of reflecting become advanced communication skills.

Effective mirroring and backtracking demonstrates your ability to witness the client as a whole person. It also simultaneously enables an increase in their awareness and learning. You will employ this tool to reflect pertinent, often game-changing information to the client in ways previously not received.

When you "mirror and backtrack" your clients, you:

- Accurately reflect key words or phrases using your client's language (especially early in the coaching relationship)

- Highlight aspects of the conversation that generate positive momentum

- Gently mirror body language and non-verbal cues to meet your client in their own world

- Act consciously in a manner that feels natural to you and the client

- Create trust, rapport, clarity and deepen understanding

Mirroring is a natural neurobiological process. Perhaps you've noticed two people in a restaurant. From afar, you sense the connection they share. Their legs are crossed in a similar fashion. They hold eye contact, mirroring each other's gestures and smiles. If you've ever worked with a counselor, therapist or coach, you may have experienced the power of mirroring and backtracking as well.

Empathy: embracing the whole

Coaching is all about creating positive momentum. But it's also about knowing when to pause and allow information and emotions to process and pass. In this sense, empathy is about recognizing the depth of impact that a given challenge or opportunity represents to someone. At the same time, it allows you to be with your clients in the most supportive ways possible.

Empathy enables you to envision what a given experience is like for someone else and adopt their perspective without taking it as your own. It's a critical relational tool that allows you to relate to other people and be an empowering presence for them. Being empathetic with another differs from the way some of us naturally react when faced with other people's strong emotions or difficult stories. When we are triggered by someone else's emotional state, we can become uncomfortable in our own bodies. Our thoughts shift. And in this discomfort, we unconsciously try to solve their problem or fix "them." At the very least, we get drawn into our own emotions and leave the conversation to tend to our own inner experiences.

When you "empathize" with your clients, you:

- Manage your own discomfort with emotions
- Invite your client to identify their own needs and ways to get them met

- Become adaptive and generative in how you view your client's situation
- Resist the need to intellectualize the conversation with logic and reasoning
- Open an invitational space for the client to process through their own emotions
- Give the client the time they need, welcoming silence

Sympathy on the other hand, is when we feel pity or sorrow for someone else's misfortune. You see hurricane or flood victims on TV who have lost their homes. Or you feel loss when you hear someone close to someone else has died. The easiest way to remember the difference is this: you have sympathy for someone; you experience empathy with someone.

As a professionally trained coach, you have an innate ability to hold a space of understanding and support for others. Your ability to be with whatever is arising inside the coaching session is what makes it possible for your clients to process difficult emotions and move into more resourceful states on their own accord. For most people, this skill alone is a game-changer to have in their personal and professional tool kits.

Empowering others

As a coach, you are in a privileged position. Your clients have chosen you as copilot on their change-making journey. Your involvement in their learning process makes it possible for them to achieve their goals. But there's a lot more to it than that. The relationship you develop with your clients holds the potential to have an even bigger impact, extending beyond the accomplishment of their goals and dreams. Your impact reaches far into the future of their lives and most important relationships.

The field of interpersonal neurobiology teaches that any significant relationship can shape an individual's mind and experiences for the better. This implies that the connection you share with your clients and the support you provide are paramount to the results you'll achieve together. Not only will they perform better, the entire process will feel easier.

Perhaps you know this feeling yourself? Think of the boost in confidence you feel when someone else supports your ideas. Or what about the second wind your bestie inspired when you ran the half marathon together?

While these moments of assurance and connection are highly effective at propelling us toward specific goals, true empowerment goes much deeper. Through the natural process of learning and brain development, we internalize the presence of others. Our brains and bodies encode memorable moments, registering information from our sensory organs. Like how you felt hearing "I love you" for the first time, or the impact harsh words from a parent attempting to keep you safe and out of trouble. This is how impactful people and significant experiences – past and present, positive and negative – come to "live" as mental representations inside our minds.

For example, notice what happens when you think about someone who has deeply touched your life. Perhaps this person was a former teacher, parent, partner or best friend. What thoughts and feelings arise? Can you hear their voice? See their facial expressions? What do you notice in terms of bodily sensations as you recall them?

In this regard, we all hold the potential to learn from those around us and become embodied by one another. As a Whole Person Coach, you have the rare opportunity to add a positive, empathetic presence into your client's life. The support you offer also holds the potential for your presence to become woven into their neural tapestry – an empowering voice within their inner world. Through the natural process of relational influence, your impact is key to your clients achieving greater confidence, compassion and self-understanding in immeasurable ways.

As someone who has worked with coaches for years, I can't begin to count the number of moments when I heard one of their voices in my head. Their impact has been so inspiring, it's often like they're standing right beside me still. They champion my success in moments of triumph. They remind me to see things differently when I struggle. I can't imagine a greater privilege or responsibility than to be someone's internal cheerleader.

Can you?

Attuning, believing, mirroring and empathy are just a few of the core relationship-building skills you will learn when you train to become a Whole Person Coach. Next up, we'll discuss a few of the communication skills you'll develop during your training.

Catalytic Communication

As a coach, your communication style is unlike the conversations you tend to hold with friends and family. Think about the last time you sat down with a friend for coffee or at a café. First, it's likely your conversation jumped from topic to topic, the agenda moving with the flow of both your interests and concerns. It's not uncommon for friends (especially close friends) to finish one another's sentences with a word or two. Or to interrupt one another and interject our own ideas. As we default to our experience, the conversation often shifts the focus back to us. But as a professional coach, your communication is focused on your client, their experience and their agenda. Your chosen method of communication creates the positive momentum necessary for them to succeed.

Catalytic Communication is the term we use to describe the game-changing and frequently life-changing conversations you engage your clients in. These exchanges elicit the insight, strategies and skillful actions people need to move from point A (their present situation) to point B (their preferred future).

There are three primary techniques in Catalytic Communication:

- Reflecting
- Witnessing
- Questioning

Together these three techniques form a conversational engine. They are also the behind-the-scenes mechanics that transform you as a coach into a highly effective communicator and influencer… even when you're not coaching.

Before jumping into the techniques of Catalytic Communication, let's look at the basics of coaching and expand from there.

Your clients come to you seeking to achieve a goal or dream. Some want to solve a problem. Others may simply want to become more effective in one or more aspects of their life. Even more seek a complete life reinvention today. Regardless of their end goal, they are currently struggling with some aspect of the status quo or their present situation. What they want is a preferred future outcome. This is where your Catalytic Communication skills come in.

These three communication styles, in combination, propel your clients from the struggles of the present moment toward their desired outcome. Each technique has its own unique role to play in the process. The dance and flow of the coaching conversation that follows is what deepens your client's self-awareness, self-acceptance, actions and accountability. It is also what ultimately produces the clarity, direction and focus they need to accomplish their goals.

Witnessing: listening and observing

While many view powerful inquiry as the primary skill in coaching, the effectiveness of the questioning process actually relies heavily on the coach's ability to attune with and fully witness the client throughout the coaching process. This is why we place these two skills at the forefront in Whole Person Coaching. Your capacity to be deeply present with your clients makes it possible for you to witness their individual depth and breadth, as well as the whole of their experiences. It allows you to gather the information necessary to affect change and bring out the best from your client and the entire coaching process.

Witnessing also validates your intuition and gut instincts, because you gain further information that backs what you're sensing from within. This information can be used to aid your clients to see more clearly and holistically for themselves. These "ah-ha" moments are one of the most powerful, rewarding aspects of serving others in this capacity.

As your clients share their stories, strategies and action steps taken thus far, your witnessing skills help you decipher what they truly need to achieve their goals. This style of listening is multidimensional. It draws upon the wisdom of the whole person in both you and your clients.

So often we simply listen to respond or seek to identify the problem. More often than not, we are also listening for what resonates within our own story, so we can jump in with a "me too." Don't get me wrong: there are certainly moments in which this style of communication is appropriate. Communication geared toward finding common ground is frequently essential. But as a coach, you are in service to the client's agenda. If you've shared a similar path, terrific! As Whole Person Coaches however, we invite our clients to self-discover their own pathway forward. This can often be different than our own experience (and it usually is). Your client leads the way, not vice versa.

As a Whole Person Coach, you witness your client as a whole person. This includes the mental, emotional, social, somatic and spiritual aspects of their being. As your clients communicate with you, they share aspects of both their internal and external experience.

This often includes:

- How they are feeling
- What they sense in their body
- What they are thinking

- Their deepest needs and motivations
- Their actions and reactions
- The environments in which they exist
- Their relationships with others
- Their inner dialog
- Their perspectives and beliefs
- Their passions and values
- Which part of their persona is driving their thought processes
- Aspects that remain unheard or unacknowledged

As your clients talk about their experience, your highly-trained ears and eyes are also taking in additional information — knowledge that lives beneath their conscious radar. This often includes what is not being said, but also encompasses the cues that are evidenced through somatic indicators such as body language or non-verbal communications.

Observing goes beyond just noticing the obvious. It assists you and your clients to identify any unknown factors that influence their capacity to achieve their goals. This may include any blind spots or conditioned tendencies they are unaware of. More importantly, you uncover the strengths and resources that have, up until now, remained invisible or untapped.

When you "witness" your clients, you:

- Uncover information that resides on and off the client's radar, lighting up blinds spots and the unconscious content relevant to their desired outcome

- Remain curious and interested in learning more from the client, versus assuming you have the answers

- Witness the whole person, including the mental, emotional, somatic, spiritual and social aspects of their being

- Separate your client's experience from your own, viewing them in their experience versus using yours as a roadmap or means of comparison

- Recognize your client's negative self-talk or other self-sabotaging habits as a symptom of an unmet need versus a problem to fix

- Focus on the client's resources, strengths and other assets, as well as any limiting beliefs or unmet needs

Once gathered, this information provides you with a deep level of insight and clarity. It can often reveal what might be your next steps in supporting the client's agenda.

Your multidimensional listening skills, empower you to learn from the whole of your client's communication. You gain a holistic perspective and far more accurate understanding about them and their process. Most important: you discover what will help them succeed.

While witnessing is key to sensing what the client and coaching process need, it is only one step in the process. A seasoned witness intuitively follows a conversation by registering the themes and patterns expressed by the client. From here, they integrate their discoveries into the flow of the conversation through a process of reflecting.

This enables your client to see what you are seeing... and potentially even more!

Reflecting: deepening awareness

No one likes uncertainty. Nor do we like the discomfort of not having the answers or clarity necessary to make sense of the things that keep us feeling lost or locked in a situation without choice. This makes your ability to sense what is invisible to others a highly valued asset in your clients' lives. Identifying it yourself is only the first step in the process though.

We've already looked at the importance of mirroring and backtracking your client's words and gestures to create trust and rapport. Reflecting is an advanced form of these skills. Reflecting allows you to introduce (and at times reintroduce) new information into the conversation while engaging your client in the process. Obtained via your client's verbal, non-verbal and visual communication, this information is the language of the mind, body, heart and spirit. Through these advanced observations, your clients gain access to a bigger picture and clearer understanding of their situation and self. They also gain access to the inner guidance and wisdom that resides within. They are now far better positioned to identify what they truly need to close the gap between where they are at and where they want to be.

What you choose to reflect may include:

- Your client's words along with your own perspective or a slight reframe
- Incongruities or conflicting viewpoints

- Polarities: black or white, either/or thinking
- Your own somatic experience of a situation
- Incongruences between words and actions
- Potential-limiting beliefs or perspectives
- Puzzling expressions or body language
- Energy that is rigid, chaotic or otherwise inhibiting their highest potential

Let's look at how witnessing and reflecting work together in the following example. A client referred her coworker to me not long ago. The coworker, who we'll call Rebecca, had recently asked her husband, Grant, for a divorce. Unfortunately, taken off guard by her sudden decision to end the marriage, Grant had become extremely passive-aggressive toward her. Recognizing that she didn't want to simply get a lawyer and throw him under the proverbial bus (there were kids involved), Rebecca was struggling with her own feelings of anger toward him. She was frustrated that Grant wasn't 'taking things in stride', despite a relationship that, for her, had been unfulfilling and often strenuous for years.

Based on what I was hearing, Grant was obviously hurt. He was doing his best to deal with her expected request for a divorce and the pending loss of his wife, family and house. In her frustration, Rebecca could only see her side, which limited her view on how she felt she could deal with her situation. The coaching conversation went something like this...

Me: "Rebecca, it sounds like you are quite unhappy with Grant's behavior toward you. You feel he is being passive-aggressive, and you're concerned about how that's affecting the kids."

Rebecca: "Yes. I'm really sick of his attitude. And it's just uncomfortable. I can't wait 'til he's out of the house. Which of course isn't going to happen until we finalize the divorce." *[flustered]*

Me: "You're frustrated, Rebecca. I can hear it in your voice and words."

Rebecca: "You bet I am. You know I've struggled with this marriage for the past three years. When I finally get the guts to ask for a divorce, he acts like he has no clue as to why I feel this way."

Me: "Sounds like he has no clue as to how you're feeling."

Rebecca: "No. But that's the story of our marriage."

At this point in the conversation, my goal was to be present with her and her feelings. Mirroring and backtracking her experience as accurately as possible. While this enriched our rapport, it also allowed her to feel heard and her needs recognized without the pressure to change anything. It also gave me the opportunity to gain a deeper understanding of her situation and what she was experiencing internally and from her husband.

The key to reflecting is to share your observations in a way that enables your client to receive the information and engage in a self-discovery process toward a more holistic viewpoint and understanding. This requires a skillful approach, especially when the topic is emotional in its subject matter or potentially reflective of the client's identity. In this situation, Rebecca was very aware of her own feelings. While she said she wanted to work things out, she was unable to recognize the link between Grant's behaviors and his own feelings. Had I tried to invite the conversation at this point toward some form of resolution, it's likely I would have been met with defensiveness. At the extreme, she may have even seen me as unsupportive of her. As our conversation progressed, her emotions began to subside. That's when I engaged her more deeply, reflecting back some of my own observations.

Me: "It sounds like this has been going on for a long time?"

Rebecca: "Yes, and no. To be honest, I'm not in love with him anymore. When we met, we were two different people. We were so young. I don't know what happened, but I'm ready to move on."

Me: "What do you want to happen right now?"

Rebecca: "I want him to be a grown-up. *[awkwardly laughs]* I want him to be civil and responsible right now. He's avoiding the whole situation."

Me: "Had the two of you talked about divorce before you asked for one?"

Rebecca: "No. I was worried he'd blow up. He never talks about his feelings, it's like they just disappear into his body. I can feel his anger, but he denies he's mad."

Me: "From everything I've heard, it sounds like you may have caught him by surprise. How do you think he felt when you asked for the divorce?"

Rebecca: "Devastated. I could tell by the look on his face."

Me: "How would you react under such conditions?"

Rebecca: "Probably the same…"

Me: "I'm hearing you want to feel comfortable being around him and for him to be cooperative with the divorce. What might he need to feel more comfortable too? It seems he too may have some unmet needs."

Rebecca: "Now, that's a good question."

In some cases, what you offer won't land for the client right away. But with patience, trust and time, eventually it will connect. We all process information in our own way. Some people need time to reflect on what they've heard before it sinks in. For example, Rebecca was unreceptive in the moment to seeing Grant in any other way. But my reflections and focus on her needs allowed her to feel heard. This brought her back into a mental state where she became more open to seeing the bigger picture.

Many coaches use the term "resistance" to describe moments like this. But in Whole Person Coaching, we consider the client merely unreceptive to the information. The reasons for this are as varied as the individuals themselves. A protective behavior may be playing out. Maybe the heat of the moment has skewed their acceptance of new information. And, as mentioned earlier, some people simply need more time or information to shift their point of view. So instead of viewing a client as "resistant," we see it as a matter of being in the right state of mind to receive additional information.

This is an area where some coaches struggle. Especially when they believe that what they are seeing is vital to the client's success (and theirs too!). As coaches, we all want to provide value. But as Whole Person Coaches, we recognize that if the client isn't ready, willing or able to take in additional information or see different options, forcing the issue only adds to their burden. Besides, you run the risk they will leave just as frustrated as they were when they sat down (if not more so). These moments offer up a unique opportunity for you to shift your approach and unattach from the idea that there is only one way results can happen or a timeline for it to happen.

Remember: the client chooses whether they accept what you're offering. Newly discovered information has a funny way of resonating in bigger and better ways with the more time that passes. Think of a snowball. It starts at the top of a mountain, no larger than a tennis ball. But with a little nudge under the right conditions (gradient, wind, temperature), that snowball could pick up momentum and eventually turn into an avalanche. When information of this sort finally does land, it often creates an even deeper impact than the client had initially hoped for. Once they're in a more receptive state, they sense the importance of it and suddenly see how it fits into the larger puzzle.

I remember a fishbowl coaching session we conducted in the classroom a few years ago. A fishbowl is where one client is coached by three to four coaches in succession.

The first coach in the process did an exceptional job of setting up the conversation for success by eliciting the client's desired outcome and session deliverable. With that in place, the client started to tell her story. Her struggles became evident within five minutes or so.

The second coach explicitly named the struggle, but the client was unable to hear it. She deflected the coach's comments and became defensive in her body language. Even though the client was open to coaching, she couldn't hear this particular information.

Yet by the time the fishbowl session had progressed to the fourth and final coach, the same observation was reflected to the client. This time, the information landed. The client recognized her role in the situation and her underlying motivations. In this game-changing moment, she shifted her perspective and felt immediate relief.

As you might guess, the second coach was confused as to why her observation, repeated almost word for word by someone else later in the conversation, was initially rejected. Why hadn't the client been able to hear it from her?

No one can truly know exactly why the client wasn't receptive in the beginning of the conversation. But several factors were likely at play:

- Timing
- Trust
- Relevancy
- Coach's delivery

Even though the second coach's intuition was on target, the timing for such valuable information wasn't right. The client wasn't in a state where she was receptive to it. Perhaps she was caught in the story and emotional undercurrent it was producing within her. Or maybe she didn't feel comfortable going in that direction at that time. In many ways, she may not have felt "safe" to explore.

And let's not forget trust. While trust may have been in place between the two students, the client's own self trust may have also played into the conversation. It could have been that she didn't feel she had the capacity to deal with the truth of her matter. Or perhaps, from her viewpoint, she didn't perceive the information to be relevant to her situation. As a result, she was initially blind to the connection the coach was making.

This can represent a big challenge in coaching, especially when a client is under stress. A person's ability to be open to additional information and perspectives is often limited, particularly when the client-coach relationship has yet to develop the necessary trust and rapport.

While the exact reason the information didn't land may never be known, the way in which you communicate with your clients is a critical element in whether or not someone listens to what you have to say or turns away.

It's worth underlying this key point: the way in which you communicate with your clients plays a huge role in their ability to receive information and even accept your questions.

You approach the world in your own distinct way, interacting with others through a communication style all your own. Yet however you prefer to approach others – whether head on or through the back door – people are far more receptive to neutral communication that comes from a place of not-knowing and curiosity. As you'll soon discover, questions and feedback that allow your clients to be at choice and fully express themselves versus communication that comes with an agenda are the key to those breakthrough moments.

When you "reflect" your clients, you:

- Share observations related to your client's agenda and desired outcome
- Paraphrase their words to create more clarity

- Comment and inquire about the meaning of their gestures, body language and tone

- Offer your own somatic or emotional impact from the conversation

- Make your observations then let the client decide what and how they'd like to use it, if at all (remember: your client always has a choice as to whether or not they use the information you offer)

- Equally engage the client to make their own observations

- Encourage your clients to develop their own inner-witness

- Relax, knowing there is a right time for everything, and allow your client to process information and insights on their own

I've been talking a lot about the use of reflection. But before we move on, it's important to realize that reflecting isn't just about offering what you are witnessing and your insights. Cultivating these skills within your client is just as important.

Using inquiry, you invite your clients to become their own witness. In other words, you assist them to self-observe through targeted questions that draw their attention to the whole of their experience, inside and out. These questions also enable them to explore their own thoughts, feelings, sensations, behaviors and actions directly. For many, this might look like the practice of mindfulness. Yet it's so much more.

Which brings us to the power of inquiry and the third and final component of Catalytic Communication:

questioning. Get ready! Because this is the point at which you often see everything fall into place.

Questioning: powerful inquiry

Powerful questions support your clients' self-discovery and learning process. Questioning empowers them to discover (and often rediscover) their own answers and resources. This is what leads them to figure it out on their own and generate positive momentum, both inside the coaching conversation and outside in their lives. Through powerful inquiry, you invite others to fully engage in a collaborative and co-creative process – one that brings out the best in you both!

As we just discussed, reflecting is the art of sharing your observations and insights with your clients. It enables them to see and hear for themselves information that is important in their change-making efforts. It's also a skill you'll develop in your clients as you engage them into their own self-discovery processes and reflective thinking. Your questions are what deepen, amplify and advance the coaching process. They assist you to move the conversation toward manifesting your client's stated goal.

As a coach, you'll employ a wide combination of inquiries. From clarifying to probing. From questions that elicit feelings and needs to others that bring about strategic or even contemplative thinking. Your exact questions form responsively to what is happening in the present moment of the conversation and the client's agenda. To better understand the basic use of questions in this process, let's venture over to the FootSteps Model.

The FootSteps Model

We use our Whole Person Coaching FootSteps model to illustrate the flow of a coaching conversation. It's a nine-step framework in which you learn the basic types of questions to facilitate your client's agenda and cultivate the awareness, learning, action and accountability necessary to manifest their goals. What follows is an insider's look at how a few powerful questions can work to create positive momentum for others.

F *ocus*

O *pportunities*

O *bstacles*

T *est*

S *hift*

T *ake action*

E *valuate*

P *rogress*

S *ustain*

Phases	Types of Questions
I. Establish the Session Focus and Deliverable	Begin the coaching session by empowering your client to take the lead. This happens as you invite them to establish a session focus and deliverable for the coaching session.
	Part 1: Create a Session Focus
	Invite your client to decide on the purpose for that coaching session by using some variation of these powerful yet open-ended questions:
	• What would you like to focus on?
	• What do you feel is most important to look at today?
	• How would you like to spend your time?
	• What's on your mind that you'd like to cover today?
	• What would you like to discuss today?
	Part 2: Create the Session Deliverable
	A few sample questions include:
	• What would you like to have as a result of our coaching session?
	• What would you like to be able to do after our coaching session?
	• How would you like to feel as a result of our coaching session?
	• Who would you like to become as a result of our coaching session?

Phases	Types of Questions
II. Explore the Client's Opportunities	From here, you'll use exploratory and probing questions to generate more clarity and understanding of your client's current situation as it relates to their session deliverable. You are listening for clues into opportunities that create positive momentum and increase motivation. *A few sample questions include:* • What has yet to be leveraged to create positive momentum? • What has already been attempted? • What do I need to know to support you with this goal? • What resources do you have in place right now related to this goal? • What have you tried thus far? • Seeing your good efforts bring about the results you were hoping for must have felt great. Can you say more about how you are feeling about your success so far? • What will you get out of having accomplished this? • It sounds like this is very important to you. On a scale of 1 to 10 how motivated are you right now? What would make it a 10?

Phases	Types of Questions
III. Explore the Client's Obstacles	Continuing your exploration, you invite your client to share with you what they believe to be the issue or problem. Ultimately what you are listening for is what they need in terms of a process or solution to move forward. That is what they feel needs to be addressed. *A few sample questions include:* • What do you think the problem is? • Watching your facial expression and your body language, it's clear you don't want to go back to this job/situation/relationship. What's preventing you from acting on these feelings? • What do you need to accomplish this? • What's stopping you? • What do you believe is the reason this is happening? • What do you believe lies beneath your challenge with this? (Exploring any limiting beliefs or outdated viewpoints – that is the story the client is in.) • What do you need in place in terms of a strategy or plan to move forward? (Inviting the creation of a strategy, map, plan or actions to move forward.) • What might you need to feel more comfortable with your chosen path? (Inviting the client to step into a more resourced state.)

Phases	Types of Questions
IV. Test-n-Tune into the Client's Needs	At this point in the conversation it's useful to synthesize what the client has expressed both explicitly and implicitly. Doing so, you can test your understanding and engage them in the process to identify their needs and a potential next step or process in the conversation.
	A few sample questions include:
	• Now that you've explored your options and the challenges or barriers you see, it sounds like you feel your biggest challenge is to _____. Where would you like our conversation to go from here?
	• As you've shared, I'm sensing you want to feel confident about what you are going to say before taking action. I'm also hearing you are concerned with how your requests will be met by _____, and that you worry it could create tension. What do you think is most important to focus on with this information in mind?
	• When you take into consideration our work thus far, what do you feel you need in this moment?
	• As you have been sharing, I noticed some energy in your voice. How are you feeling after hearing this? What does that mean to you? How would you like to address this?
	• I'm hearing that you are conflicted. One part of you wants the freedom of working on your own. The other part wants the security of a paycheck. How do you feel about exploring these needs from a different perspective?

Phases	Types of Questions
V. Shift to Solutions (Inviting the Self-Innovation)	Often considered the tipping point in the conversation, this vital phase builds upon the "FOOT"ing that has been created thus far in the conversation. Your goal is to pivot the focus of the conversation from exploration toward meeting the client's needs as discussed. While there are no specific types of questions you'll employ at this point in the process, it's likely your process will flow to address: • The client's story - supporting the client to identify and shift any limiting perspectives or beliefs that hold them back. • The client's strategies - assisting the client to address any self-sabotaging habits while strengthening resourceful ones. • The client's state - inviting the client to step into a resourced state of mind and into their deepest potential. As a Whole Person Coach, you are equipped with a number of tools and techniques that allow you to fully customize a coaching approach unique to your client's needs and your preferred way of working with them.. Once they've worked through any stopping blocks and have amplified their strengths and resourcefulness, you invite them into the next phase to take action.

Phases	Types of Questions
VI. Client Takes Action	In this next phase, you invite your client to take what they are learning back out into their world. You encourage them to commit to skillful action steps and an accountability structure. Typically you would backtrack the flow of the conversation first then shift into questions. *A few sample questions include:* • What's your first action here? • How might you take what you are learning out into this situation? • What's most important for you to accomplish next? • How will you stay on track? • What might you need to remain accountable to your goals? • What would you like to accomplish before our next session?

Phases	Types of Questions
VII. Evaluate the Action and Coaching Process	This next step is two-fold. It's about you receiving feedback to hone your skills. But it's also about the client evaluating their work inside and outside of the coaching session.
	It enables you to adapt your coaching style to better serve the client. Same goes for the client: if they notice their present course isn't working, this is the time to self-reflect on how to improve.
	A few sample questions include:
	• How do you feel about your progress?
	• What worked? What didn't?
	• How might you shift your approach?
	• Are you still feeling on track with your desired outcome?
	• How are you feeling about your success?
	• How might the coaching process support you in your process?
	• How might I be even more effective as your coach?

Phases	Types of Questions
VIII. Progress to the Finish Line	In this phase, you invite your client to generate new strategies or micro-adjustments to improve their process and stay on course to successfully achieve their goals. *A few sample questions include:* • It sounds like the way in which you've been attempting to reach your goals has not produced the results you want. What does this information tell you about your process? What changes would you like to make? • How might you enhance your progress? • Is there something you haven't tried that could make this easier? • What might be an even more strategic way to approach your desired outcome? • Are there any resources you might draw upon to reach your goal more easily?

Phases	Types of Questions
VIIII. Sustain the Learning	Lastly, you'll want to take your client's learning into new depths by helping them see their brilliance and recognize their own capacity for self-innovation. This last step locks in the lessons learned and shows them how easily they can use the tools to manifest change in any other process or aspect of life. *A few sample questions include:* • How might what you are learning serve you in the future? • With all that you've discovered, what is most important for you to remember? • What are you learning today that might be useful in your future? • What do you notice about yourself, and what might that mean for your future? • It really feels like you've come to a whole new way of understanding yourself. How might you leverage this new knowing in other areas of your life? *Hint: A victory dance to celebrate your mutual success is never a bad idea at this point!*

Although it's presented here in linear format for demonstration, the FootSteps Model is rarely reflective of the actual coaching conversation itself, which is more akin to a dance. It's merely a glimpse of what the structure might look like in a linear fashion. Consider it a backbone upon which you can architect the ideal coaching process, meeting your clients with who they are and recognizing their natural learning styles and strengths.

You may have already noticed: the potential for questions is endless. Many students want a cheat sheet containing the best questions to ask their clients. This is contrary to the concept of Whole Person Coaching in which each coaching session is unique to the client and their natural learning and processing styles. Success comes from your capacity to offer a highly creative process. We'll be demonstrating this process in more detail within the next chapter.

It's a lot of moving parts. But when they come together, there is no faster, more effective way to impact the lives of those you choose to serve.

By leveraging the FootSteps model to sync with your clients, you elicit highly effective conversations that maximize your client's time, efforts and capacity to realize their desired changes. These conversations spark a deeper sense of self-knowing and responsibility to one's deepest desires and inner truth. They allow people to see their wholeness and step into their greatest capacities.

Your coaching excels as a result. You become the go-to resource who reliably elicits change at a deeper and thus sustainable level, delivering on what people expect of you… and quite often exceeding those expectations.

Coaching skills aren't just for coaches

Your enhanced coaching communication skills don't just benefit your clientele. A notable side-benefit is frequently seen by all those around you. Others soon notice your capacity to effectively communicate and navigate difficult conversations. You notice it too. Soon, you'll be deftly and automatically shifting away from those draining conversations. The ones where, no matter what approach you take, you always end up where you began.

That's because your communication skills "rub off" on those around you, providing further benefit to you as a coach, as well as those you cherish most. Friends, family, coworkers and even bosses experience your enhanced communication skills.

It's not uncommon for a coach-in-training to find themselves with a promotion at work. And I can't count the number of coaches who suddenly realize their clients, children, spouses and lifelong friends have changed their own communication style from negative or limiting phrases to life-affirming language simply because of their interactions with the coach in their life.

But as mentioned, we are just dipping our toes into coaching's deep potential to affect change in your life and the lives of others.

Chapter review and coming attractions

In this chapter, you got a glimpse of what it looks to be a Whole Person Coach, both for you and your clients. You discovered the basics of co-creating an empowering coaching relationship and some of the communication skills you'll employ to generate momentum. You also learned about the FootSteps process! Your relationship and communication skills are the foundation of your work as a coach.

Next Up: We'll take a deeper look into what makes this holistic process truly transformational for both you and your clients. You'll witness how you can use this approach to work with the depth of human nature, creating exponential transformations in individuals and business alike.

~ *In Your Journal* ~

The following somatic information can help you understand yourself and your experiences related to this moment, and how it feels to explore Whole Person Coaching.

- Do a gut check. Notice what you are feeling right now in your body. If it helps, place one hand on your belly and the other on your heart. Whatever is true for you, take note.

- Now take note of your thoughts. What's on your mind? How do your thoughts reflect what you are feeling in your body? In your heart?

- Finally, call upon your higher power, whether it's your own inner-knowing, a spiritual connection to source, God, or your own preference. Notice the connection you hold and feel into this connection as you consider coaching others.

~4~

Innovate Here: Whole Person Coaching

Accelerate your success with a tailor-made,
holistic approach for evoking sustainable
change: working with the whole person.

We use the lotus in Whole Person Coaching for its
rich symbolism. Delicate yet unyielding, it links
transformation and a person's capacity to emerge into the
whole of who they are through coaching. Lotus flowers
grow out of dark, murky waters yet produce beautiful
white and pink blossoms. They are considered a symbol
of strength within adversity and representative of our
capacity to rise from a dark place into immense beauty,
strength and resourcefulness. Through this darkness
and uncertainty – a state we can all relate to at times – we

learn to grow and develop as we reconnect and return to our wholeness and fullest potential.

Take a moment to imagine yourself as a tiny lotus seed, whole and complete. You are buried deep in the mud at the center of a murky pond. Although your surroundings are dirty and the pathway unclear, your journey is to navigate through the darkness and travel into the light where you can fully emerge. Above the surface, the clarity you desire awaits.

You begin to wrestle about within the confines of your pod, cracking your tiny prison until you break through. Your roots extend below into the soft nourishment of a highly supportive partnership – someone who holds faith and trust in your capacity. Someone who sees your potential, often long before it is visible even to you.

Called forth by the light of who you are, your stem journeys forth, making its way to the water's surface. Up, up, up you travel, through unclear and often dark waters. Until at last, you draw upon your greatest strengths and deepest wisdom, rising above the water's surface.

Now in the light, possessing a deep sense of inner knowing, the trust and certainty you embody provide the stability and structure from which you can fully emerge. Your lotus bud is in bloom, fragrant and full. You are now in stark contrast to your muddy beginnings, standing tall and radiant above the pond far below. As the lotus, you represent the fullest expression of your wholeness. You have blossomed into the truest and fullest version of yourself.

Through Whole Person Coaching, your clients accomplish their goals and manifest their dreams. They also rise above outdated or inhibited versions of themselves.

This transformation empowers them to create holistic, sustainable change that becomes exponential in other areas of their life as well. The process you offer employs self-actualization as a key component to accomplishing their goals and dreams. Like a lotus flower, they rise into the whole of who they truly are, fully and freely expressed in a life of their choosing.

In the last chapter, we discussed the foundational elements in your change-mastery skill set. In this chapter, we'll explore the process of change mastery through several case studies. My intention is to show you Whole Person Coaching (WPC) in action, imparting actual examples of its adaptability and wide-ranging application.

Light the way

As a Whole Person Coach, you facilitate a transformational learning journey. This is accomplished through a tailor-made process customized to reflect your unique expertise and designed to meet the true needs and desired outcome of your clients. It is also the product of your perceptiveness. Your training as an astute witness empowers you to easily recognize your client's underlying mental and emotional activities. This includes habitual thinking, emotional impacts and the belief systems in your client's narrative that contour their ability (for better or worse) to be successful in their endeavors.

To bring your discoveries to light, you employ a selected combination of mindfulness-based tools and somatic practices. They help your clients listen to and draw upon the multiple intelligences that reside within as they come to know their deep and powerful nature. Through this elevated awareness, their blind spots are exposed and they are able to operate from a tremendous advantage: clarity. Not only does their untapped potential become visible, any conscious and unconscious self-sabotaging patterns are also revealed. This new comprehension gives them the insight necessary to unlock from the patterns of habit no longer serving them. From there, you champion them as they transcend the previously-unknown roadblocks and barriers to their success, now thriving inside and out.

The resulting deep-seated self-knowledge enables your coaching clients to make new choices. Their actions align with their truest nature (and best pathway forward!). Even better, they do so regardless of previous influences and experiences. Better still, your efforts work at a level shared by all persons regardless of social, intellectual or cultural influences. This is what makes your coaching as a Whole Person Coach universally applicable.

But this wakened state is only part of the shift. A secondary element occurs as your clients come to recognize the nature and influence of their inner and outer experiences, and the story that forms in-between. They discover the interrelated nature of the core content that shapes the stories they live in: thoughts, feelings, images and sensations, in concert with the results they are achieving.

This self-recognition allows them to feel more comfortable to explore their learning edges and reveals any patterns that have kept them from being at their best. Their new-found freedom is a direct product of the courageous space you've co-created, as well as your ability to hold a space of curiosity and comfort with them and their process. Additionally, your process facilitates their ability to be non-judgmental and compassionate with themselves and others. This is another main contributor to moving your clients past their roadblocks and into action on the path that will serve them best.

While awareness and acceptance are inextricably linked, I would argue the latter is more important. This is where change happens… or not. Through self-acceptance and compassion, your client's mind-space expands. As the inner conflict passes and emotions resolve, they become more open, creative and receptive to new perspectives. This includes new ways of seeing themselves and their situation. And it often leads to those life-enhancing breakthrough moments we all come to know and love (coach and client alike).

Now let's take a look at what is possible with examples from a few real-life coaching clients…

Meet Alex: passion on the mind

With his brilliant intellect and hardworking nature, Alex had found a fast track to success. He loved his work, the exhilaration of climbing to the top at the advertising agency, and the gratification of the financial rewards and respect he was garnering. But now, after twenty years in a job where he was both an established expert and a leader in his industry, Alex was facing one of the biggest decisions of his career.

Alex came to me after receiving a request to speak with senior management about his position. He sought insight into the ambivalence he felt about his work and life in general. Engaging him as a whole person, our conversation went like this:

Me: "Alex, you've just shared that you have a meeting tomorrow you're concerned about. I can hear part of you is worried about what the meeting is really about, and the other part is hoping it will set you in a new direction with your life. Where do you want to be as a result of our conversation today?"

Alex: "I feel like I'm out to sea right now. I should be happy. I should be thankful. *[Said in self-disgust.]* I make more money and receive more accolades than most of my peers and colleagues. I feel guilty for feeling this way."

Me: "What way?"

Alex: "That I don't want to be here. I'm not excited about this job anymore, and I just don't know what else to do."

Me: "And if you did know what else you might do? How would you feel?"

Alex: "I'd feel elated. I assume I'd be doing whatever 'it' is. I want to find my passion again!"

Me: "Okay. It sounds like you want to find your passion again? Is that what you'd like to focus on today?"

Alex: "Yes."

Me: "And with that focus on finding your passion in mind, what would you like to have in place as a result of our conversation?"

Alex: "My passion." *[He jokes.]* "Ok, I'd have a direction to follow that puts me closer in line with my passion."

Me: "A direction to follow? Do you mean something that you'd like to pursue work-wise?"

Alex: "Exactly."

Me: "Tell me Alex, where does your passion come from?"

Alex: "I'm talking about the real kind of passion. *[Touches his chest.]* There's no juice left in me. For the first time in years, I have to pull myself out of bed every morning. I even look forward to Fridays."

Me: "How long has this been going on?"

Alex: "Longer than I care to admit. If I'm honest, about two years now. In the beginning, I thought it was because of the new direction the company had taken. I went from working from home most of the time to being required to work at the office. I can work from home on Fridays, which is awesome. But we've grown so big, it's just not the same company anymore."

Me: "Sounds like you had more freedom before the company was bought?"

Alex: "That's a great way of putting it. Yes, more freedom with where I did my work. But more than that, more freedom in *what* I did at work too."

Me: "Can you say more about 'what you did at work'?"

Alex: "As a small company, we all wore a lot of different hats. My job was exciting – I didn't have a single role. And I didn't sit alone behind a computer most of the day either. Depending on the day, I could be training others in the company, presenting at trade shows and similar industry functions, or working with clients and the team as a creative director. When time permitted, I'd even get to contribute to some of the project designs with my knowledge of Photoshop and Illustrator. The whole experience was more than just fulfilling, it was fun. Now I'm managing paperwork and watching the clock tick as my time passes by."

Me: "Sounds like you enjoyed having a more entrepreneurial role within the company? It also feels to me like you're tired of watching your time pass by?"

Alex: "Yes. Yes."

Me: "...and staying with this company has brought you many rewards and some recognition too? That seems important to you as well?"

Alex: "I do like being seen for my efforts. Doesn't everyone?"

Me: "Yes, that certainly does feel good. You also mentioned you wanted to find your passion again. How will you know when you have it back?"

Alex: "Pretty simple – I'd feel it inside. And I'd be thrilled to be going to work again."

Me: "You know what you want! What do you feel you need to reclaim it?"

Alex: "I don't know. I'm so conflicted. On one hand, I've been at the same job for decades. It pays really well, and it used to feed my creative soul. On the other hand, I'm worried that I might be missing out on something better. That 'next level'. Do you know what I mean?"

Me: "Yes. [I touch my chest.] If you tapped into the wisdom of your heart, what might you find?"

Alex: "I kinda hope I get fired." *[With a deadpan look.]*

Me: "Fired? Your heart wishes for you to get fired?" *[Puzzled.]*

Alex: "No. Not really, but I'm thinking about it. I haven't been called into my boss's office for over a year. In many ways, I feel like I don't exist. They must really trust me, or they're just oblivious. Getting fired would give me no other option but to move on."

Me: "So you want to move on, and you are waiting for a permission slip?"

Alex: "If someone else says, 'Move on,' it's just easier. I guess you are right, it's a permission slip. I need to be excused. It's pretty awkward, I'll be in the boardroom and they just look at me. No one says anything, but I can feel it. I don't want to let anyone down."

Me: "I can tell you want to do the right thing. Who needs to write that permission slip?"

Alex: "I do." *[He goes silent for a long minute, sits back and lets out a big sigh.]* "But I just can't. With everything I have in place related to my career status and lifestyle, it could be a costly mistake. I'd never find a job like this again."

Me: "Would you be willing to try on another perspective?"

Alex: "Sure."

Me: "I'd like to invite you into a creative approach to view your situation. Ready? Imagine you're about to write that permission slip from three different viewpoints – first your head, then your heart, then your gut. But before you go there, I'd like you to pause and imagine this response literally coming out of your forehead, then out from the depth of your heart, and finally straight from the middle of your gut. Really tap into your body wisdom, okay?"

Alex: "Hmm. That's a unique set of questions. You're gonna make me think, huh?" *[Chuckles awkwardly.]*

Me: "Perhaps a little more than think, I'd like you to feel. I'm hearing a lot of conflict inside of your mind.

Why don't you stand up and engage your body in this process? I'll join you."

[We both stand up. I gently touch my forehead and mirror to him to do the same.]

Alex: "I don't normally think this way, but here it goes!" *[Taps his forehead.]* "My head says, 'Man, are you crazy? All that time you've spent getting to the top! What are you thinking?' That's the noisiest part of me. I'm tortured by conflicting thoughts twenty-four hours a day, not knowing what to listen to. I feel a bit crazy."

Me: "Twenty-four hours a day? Anything else from your mind's point of view that needs to be heard?"

Alex: "Anything else?" *[He goes silent.]* "Yes. This internal conflict is exhausting." *[He sits back down, and I follow.]*

Me: "I can imagine. It sounds like a wiser part of you is done with all the chaos of this decision. Do you feel ready to tap into a different way of viewing your situation? Your head feels exhausted."

Alex: "That would be a firm yes."

Me: "Okay. Drop down into your heart. And your heart says…" [I place my hand over my heart and gesture Alex to follow. He hesitates and then places his hand on his chest.]

Alex: "My heart says, 'You've lost that loving feeling." *[Says this humorously, mocking the song and gesturing romantically, then slumping back into place.]*

Me: "Ahh…You've lost that loving feeling. Alex, how does it feel to listen to your heart?" [I laugh at his humor. He smiles, but quickly shifts back into a more serious state.]

Alex: "It's not practical. It's what dreamers do."

Me: "It's not practical? Who else listens to their heart besides dreamers?"

Alex: "People that aren't worried about their future."

Me: "What kind of people are they?'

Alex: "Well, children for one. They don't have to worry because someone else is taking care of them. As adults, we don't have that opportunity."

Me: "Sounds like you believe that you don't have that opportunity?"

Alex: "Feels like it."

Me: "It also feels like the part of you that is offering this wisdom is your inner critic?"

Alex: "You are right."

Me: "I was hoping you'd invite your heart's perspective into the conversation."

Alex: "Yeah."

Me: "A few minutes ago, you were saying you wanted to tap into your passions. It also sounded like you wanted something to happen that would allow you to break free from your current mold."

Alex: "True. Now you can see my struggle."

Me: "Yes, it appears you've defaulted back to a more worrisome place? What happened that took you back?"

Alex: "I don't know. I think it goes back to the money thing. I've worked hard for what I've got. Plus, my family would be impacted."

Me: "Yes, you have worked hard. But it seems to me that the shift you'd like most would allow you to have it all – your passion back without a loss of money or your hard work."

Alex: "Good luck with that."

Me: "Well, you have good luck. And with another perspective, you could have it all. I'd like to check in. How are you feeling about our exploration right now?"

Alex: "I'm feeling a bit tense."

Me: "Ok, where in your body do you feel that?"

Alex: "My gut. My gut just feels all tied up in knots – FEAR, FEAR, FEAR – that old fear feeling."

Me: "That old feeling?"

Alex: "Yes. Whenever I want to venture into something new but don't know the exact outcome, my mind goes into overdrive."

Me: "Lots of thinking about your thinking?"

Alex: "Yes. I'm really good at it."

Me: "You are. In fact, it's your ability to "think" that got you to the top of your company. May I offer an observation?

Alex: "Sure."

Me: "When you tapped into your head, I heard a lot of logic and reasoning as to why you shouldn't take a step toward your passions."

Alex: "Yep. Mind over matter. Mind over everything. Think smart equals right."

Me: "And when I asked you to tap into your heart, your response came from what felt like a critical voice within your mind."

[Alex nods in agreement.]

Me: "But it also sounded like your heart was heckling you, helping you recognize the loss of that 'loving feeling'. Where's that coming from?"

Alex: "The part of me that says, 'What if you're wrong? What if work *should* be fun, like it was? I need to feel okay with this decision.'"

Me: "How does it feel to listen to that part of you? The one that says, 'what if you're wrong?'"

Alex: "I think that's the inner conflict. What if I'm holding myself back from something even better? And what if it doesn't work out?"

Me: "Great questions, Alex. What if you are holding yourself back? You had shared earlier you hoped this meeting would set you into a new direction?"

Alex: "True."

Me: "Sounds like if someone else did the dirty work and set you free, that would be OK?"

Alex: "Not really."

Me: "I'm also curious about your gut pounding out in fear. What would help you feel okay."

Alex: "The answer."

Me: "The answer. What would be the best perspective to hold to get that answer?"

Alex: "The one that allows me to make a decision? I'm really not trying to be difficult here. It's just not that simple."

Me: "You're right, it's not that simple. Let's stand back up and get the juices flowing." *[We both stand.]* "I remember a story you told me about when you first got into advertising. Do you remember that one? I believe you said you were twenty-seven at the time?"

Alex: "Yes."

Me: "Alex, I'd like you to act as if you are the twenty-seven-year-old version of yourself right now and about to step into your next career. If it helps to visualize sitting at your desk, do so – your Macintosh displaying the artwork you are about to show your first corporate client. Can you recall the feeling of joy when your boss calls you into the office for a promotion?" *[I reflect back parts of what I remember from the original story.]* "Go there now and enliven that memory from within. Once you are in that wonderful feeling, ask yourself, 'What do I really want?' I'll remain quiet until you speak."

Alex: *[Closes his eyes and takes a deep breath. His facial expression undulates between what appears to be different thinking states.]* "Well, if I'm honest, I'd like to do something more meaningful... an idea I've been mulling around with my wife. I'd like to work with the next generation. Help them gain the confidence and skills they need to succeed in the advertising world. I'd like to be more of a mentor than a manager. I think it would be fun to help young artists get a head start. I was envisioning a marketing and advertising trade school. Maybe it could be a non-profit?" *[Alex opens his eyes. He is relaxed and grounded in his words.]*

Me: "You feel confident about this idea to me."

Alex: "I think it's a great idea. No one is doing it either."

Me: "That's the entrepreneurial spirit! And what a fantastic way to employ those decades of wisdom and skills you've earned. On a gut level, how does that feel to be helping young adults, in your own trade school, sharing your experience and expertise?"

Alex: "Like being a little kid. Free. Curious. Happy. Creative again."

Me: "Yeah! Creative again. This sounds like a fantastic way for you to be passionate again?"

Alex: *[The remaining skepticism visibly leaves him, transforming his facial expression and body language.]* "Yeah… I suppose it would."

Me: "I'm noticing you are coming alive in this idea. How are you feeling about this idea overall?"

Alex: "I think it's good. The kids would totally benefit by having a place to learn the trade while picking up on-the-job experience. In my opinion, having expert mentors and real projects to work on would be refreshing to the academic ways of learning the trade. They'd learn how to develop their intuition, but also their listening skills. That is so important in this profession. Really understanding people, cultures, missions, visions…."

Me: "As you say this, what else is coming up for you?"

Alex: "I think it's a great idea. But I don't know where the money will come from. It would certainly bring more joy into my work."

Me: "Great, more joy! How do you feel in your body right now?"

Alex: *[Big sigh]* "I don't feel anything. Well, maybe a little peaceful."

Me: "Peaceful good?"

Alex: "Peaceful, with a slight edge. The good kind of edge, like I can't wait to explore this further with my wife."

Me: "So it sounds like your next step is to talk to your wife? Anything else you want to take action on?"

Alex: "Nope. She's my go-to gal. We make all our decisions together."

Me: "Ok, sounds like a plan. Anything else you'd like to talk about?"

Alex: "Nope. For now, I'm all good."

Me: "Anything that might get in your way of exploring this further with your wife?"

Alex: "Nope. She's been pretty supportive of me around this. Like I said, this job situation has been affecting my whole family."

Unlike conventional modalities, Whole Person Coaching relies on Catalytic Communication techniques. This process assists clients generate the awareness, action and accountability necessary to achieve their goals. As demonstrated in the coaching conversation above, your inquiry invites clients to holistically evaluate and understand their current story. From there, they spawn creative new ways to view themselves and their situation. Within this framework, clients like Alex move quickly beyond their fear-fueled stories and into authentic, self-directed change.

During our coaching session, Alex's inner critic had a strong hold. He was stuck inside a left-hemisphere viewpoint of logic and reasoning. Listening from our mind's perspective, we often rationalize until the heart caves in. We validate our thinking through beliefs, many of which are invalid yet remain good reasons to consider. Alex had a lot of good points. He might have to start over, might not make the same money, might…, might…, might. The list was extensive, yet nothing was the absolute truth. However, that did not prevent him from getting hooked into the logic of his rational mind – a self-imposed limbo he'd been stuck in for quite some time.

Recognizing the heavy hand of his inner critic on Alex's personal story, I invited him into a more holistic viewpoint.

This insight incorporated two additional sources of knowing: his heart and gut. Through this broader perspective, his greater wisdom began to arise. But as you noticed, his inner critic remained strong. That's when I chose to invite him into a more curious and open state, accessing a younger version of himself. This took him back to a place where he could connect more freely to his passion.

Not one… not two… but *three* brains

We have three brains. There's evidence. Researchers Grant Soosalu and Marvin Oka are developing the new field of multiple Brain Integration Techniques (mBIT)[1]. They've compiled convincing evidence of three distinct

1 Soosalu, Grant, and Marvin Oka. 2012. *mBraining: Using Your Multiple Brains to Do Cool Stuff*. CreateSpace Independent Publishing Platform.

complex neural networks. Their theories rely on such far-flung sources as embryology, neuroscience, neuro-linguistics, behavioral modeling, cognitive theory, anthropology, clinical medicine and ancient wisdom traditions such as Yoga, Taoism and Buddhism.

As we observed in Alex, the cephalic brain (head), cardiac brain (heart), and the enteric brain (gut) comprise wisdom. Or as we call it: the embodied intelligence of the whole person.

As a Whole Person Coach, you develop and nurture the holistic connection between these multiple aspects. In Alex's case, it was literally his head, heart and gut accessed through inquiry and physiology. Had the situation warranted a less verbal approach, I would have employed one or more coaching tools based in mindfulness and invited him to connect with his own inner-narrative through somatic language.

This isn't standard stuff. The ability to shift with the moment has had a tremendous impact on Whole Person Coaches and their clients alike. Pivoting your approach to meet the needs of the coaching client and situation is one of the advancements Whole Person Coaching brings to the industry.

In his next session, Alex reported that, to his surprise, the all-important meeting was about a co-worker who was planning to leave the company. The senior executives believed Alex should be the first to know since the weight of the increased workload would fall on him. After his conversation with his wife, he finally felt at peace with his decision to leave his job and start his own company. The revelation at the meeting only amplified his clarity, reinforcing that he was on the right path, both for himself and his family.

A few months later, Alex found a position in a new agency. During his interview, he pitched his marketing program for young adults, ABC: Agency Boot Camp — a concept that gave him an edge and most likely won him the job. In his new role as chief creative officer, he would lead a team nurturing young designers and marketing professionals, ages 18 to 25. Alex had found his dream business within a dream company. Though his new business didn't turn into self-employment, he still reached his desired outcome. And he did so by connecting to his passions.

Meet Jerry: liberation to get back into the good life

Jerry was no stranger to life's big changes. Nevertheless, he'd remained trapped in an extremely uncomfortable place – one he described as living at "the bottom of the canyon." Lost in a mental battlefield of indecision, he was torn between whether to retire or grow his business and sell it for a profit. The strain relentlessly plagued him with worst-case imagined future-life scenarios.

Jerry represents one of many individuals who confront "not knowing" how to move ahead into life's unknown territories. In Jerry's case, this was his third chapter.

After a series of conversations with friends, colleagues and his health and wellness team, Jerry took a leap of faith and invested in himself. He came to me feeling hopelessly stuck and seeing no way out (or so it seemed).

During our first meeting, Jerry's enthusiasm and spirit exuded the energy of a champion. He quickly offered a handshake accompanied by his naturally playful nature. But something was amiss. His questioning eyes and easily diverted attention spoke loudly. Soon I learned just how bleak Jerry believed his future to be.

A successful business owner for fourteen years, he'd been hit hard during the economic downturn. And he wasn't taking it lightly. To make matters worse, he'd lost interest in his business. With no financial reward in sight, he had become rigidly focused on financial security. Meanwhile, he was also searching for something else. The conflict that had arisen had become almost too much to bear. But here is where Jerry is different from many people. He knew better than to keep struggling alone or, worse yet, continue to drift. Despite being wrought with negative thoughts and feelings of hopelessness, he did what he knew was best: he got the support he needed.

Linger too long and life steps in

Jerry got caught in the fast lane of his business, even though his passion had deserted him years before. In place of meaningful work, productivity and efficacy became his focus. And was he ever good at his craft! Even if the work didn't engage him on a personal level, Jerry made it meaningful by being his absolute best, perfecting every detail.

Eventually, he was renowned for his work in pest identification, as well as his eagle-eye for spotting water damage and other issues that could represent costly repairs. He was a master at identifying those vital details for home buyers and looking out for their future investment. His personal mission was to inform buyers so they could make the right choice to meet their needs. Jerry was adored for his gift of detail and the humor he used to share his findings, even when the news wasn't what his clients had hoped for. Agents trusted him. And discerning home buyers sought out his careful attention.

Jerry: "I have containers inside my garage filled with the various pests that I've found in houses over the years. These bugs can literally eat through a home and cause thousands of dollars in damage. Most people don't notice this 'til it's too late. I don't want them to suffer and regret their purchase." [He shares with a smile.]

Me: "Jerry, I can see that you put yourself out there at the highest level for your clients, but it sounds like something is 'bugging' you personally? [We both giggle.] What brings you here today? What would you like to accomplish?"

Jerry: "Well, I was referred by someone who said you could help me get unstuck. I've been working in my business for a very long time. I've hired professional helpers like you before, and it's worked."

Me: "Great! Let's make it work again – you ready to get started?"

Jerry: "Let's do this."

Me: "Ok… Based on what you shared with me earlier, I think I'm clear that you'd like to decide whether you'll retire or rev up the business. What do I need to know to be able to help you at my best?"

Jerry: "Well, it sounds like you are inviting a story and it could take a while – you got time?"

Me: "Is it a good one? OK, I'll listen as long as you agree to let me know what you want for the happy ending…"

Keep in mind: there is always potential for a happy ending. Even if someone feels hopeless, they are not. Maybe a little stuck, but there is always another option, another choice – and often more than one – in most situations.

Jerry's face danced as his story revealed the numerous attempts he had made to find a way out of his predicament. He was extremely self-aware, and a proud, devoted lifelong learner. He recognized that the never-ending feeling of going nowhere had infiltrated his confidence as well as his ability to move into his next phase of life.

Jerry: "You know I used to be a youth pastor, and this conversation feels pretty familiar to me."

Me: "Sounds like you have some wisdom to draw upon already?"

Jerry: "It's always easier to help others."

Me: "Can be, but I have a feeling you already have some ideas within you. They're just not obvious… yet!"

As our conversation deepened, he jovially danced between being worried about the unknown state of his business and life as a whole. Humor played a huge part in his personality. It made him a likable guy. But as he joked and marveled about his "silly" life predicament, he'd also consistently remark how physically exhausted he felt. He was uncomfortable mentally, emotionally, physically, socially and spiritually.

Jerry: "You are right. I'm certain I have some ideas, but most of them aren't serving me well." *[Jerry launches into a story about how he ended up becoming a home inspector, detailing out the ups and downs of the business.]*

Me: "Thank you for the story. It wasn't as long as I had imagined. You must be holding back." *[We both laugh.]* "Now to our agreement – what is your happy ending?

What do you want to create for yourself and your life as a whole?"

Jerry: "Well *[big sigh]*, now that I am in my mid-sixties, I have a lot riding on the comfort and financial security of my future. I have no options. This economic downturn has really racked my business, and I'm also my own worst critic. But in the past couple of years, what's been hitting me is retirement. This is it! This is my last shot! I feel the need to really plan, really think this out – make good decisions. I can't let the short-term thrill of 'Oh I'm going to Europe on a ski trip for two weeks' cloud my thinking. I've begun looking at life long-term. I just need a plan and a process to rev up this business, so I can sell it and retire."

Jerry loved the great outdoors. Often commenting on his hundred-mile bike rides and all-day cross-country ski races, he was no stranger to the gym and the importance of health. Yet even that was starting to be affected by worries about his business and future.

Me: "What do you need to be able to retire?"

This question propels him into listing all the elements he wants to accomplish to increase the volume of his business. We end up with a to-do list that has more than thirty items. Upon seeing that, he falls back into his seat with a look of disdain.

Me: "Anything else?"

[Secretly, I can feel something seeking to emerge. His body language and facial expressions of disgust and frustration are shadowing his productive act of listing.]

Jerry: "Nope, that's it – the money that'll buy me security for my retirement."

[At this point, I'm hoping the puzzled look on my face doesn't show through. I can tell on a whole different level: this list isn't enough. But I can also tell he is not ready to consider other options.]

Me: "How will you know when you've reached your financial goal to retire?"

Jerry: "I'll believe it when I feel it... and my CPA says so." *[He thumps his chest.]* "I'll know when I know."

Me: "Sounds good – I believe you! You've had your hand on your belly during most of our conversation. Why might that be?"

Jerry: "Oh, it feels good to have it there. I think it's comforting. I didn't notice."

Me: "Got it. Sounds like you'll feel peace inside with this knowing. I'm counting on you to announce it at the very moment you realize it. Are you ready to start working toward that knowing and feeling?"

Jerry: "Sure – what do I _have to_ do?"

In Whole Person Coaching, we look at the whole person from the perspective of balance and integration of one's intellectual, emotional, physical, social and spiritual selves. The exact definitions of these elements are uniquely defined by the client. That's what makes the WPC process holistic in every step.

Prior to his business, Jerry had spent four and half years studying to be a catholic priest. During that time, he traveled all over the United States in a variety of spiritually-centered, service-based roles that had given him a keen sense of his spiritual self. As he transitioned, he moved into construction and later into home inspection. He was a natural at using his intellect to problem-solve and evaluate homes. Jerry was meticulous in the attention given to every detail. His devotion to several sports, ranging from road biking to cross country skiing, kept his body in tip-top shape. But he had become stuck intellectually, conflicted between what he really wanted and what he felt he had to do to survive the changes in the economy. This conflict was creating a lot of emotional noise and experiences, emboldening his inner critic.

Recognizing the disconnect between what he said he wanted and what his body and emotional language shared, I chose to invite the power of positivity in to manufacture some momentum (build a more resourceful state). From there, I invited him to connect to all of who he was – especially his passion and greater purpose.

Me: "Jerry, you are amazing at problem-solving. And I'm guessing it's quite the advantage to really notice the details in those homes you inspect. May I invite you to leverage those skills for some introspection? This might seem a bit off-purpose, but I promise to tie it all together in just a bit." *[Acknowledging his need to know what's coming down the pipeline, I bargain for some self-exploration.]*

Jerry: "Ok."

Me: "I'd like you to tell me a story about a time in your life when you felt really alive. Maybe one of those magical moments where life couldn't be any better!"

Jerry: "Another story?"

Me: "Yes, a positive one this time, where you are at your best, loving yourself, your life – a story about a time where everything felt right. One when you are intellectually, emotionally, physically and spiritually at your very best."

Jerry: "Well, what comes to mind is the many times when I go work on the trails in the mountains..."

Jerry goes on to paint an emotional landscape of the blissful feelings he got when he was outdoors, playing in the woods and snow, working on various cross-country ski trails. In this setting, he was spending time in nature, with good friends, often teaching others and carefully tending to the trails that served thousands of people as they sought their own peak experiences on the mountain. His carefully chosen words and the levity and lightness of his energy throughout the story, in combination with his permanent grin, was remarkably sweet. Delighting in his story, I could feel the tension dissipate. And upon completion, a total shift in energy occurred. Jerry was finally in a resourceful state, emotionally and mentally. He spoke of the spiritual connection he felt to the land, to God and to himself. Being active made him happy, compounded by the emotional satisfaction of doing what he loved and sharing it with others. He felt whole and, as a result, was in his happiest place – literally and holistically.

Me: "Jerry, where did you just go in that story?"

Jerry: "To the mountains, where I love being, in the open air, calm and at peace in nature."

Me: "And what about inside your head and body?"

Jerry: "Oh! You meant the inner world? I was really in a happy place. Positive. That's what you said to focus on."

Me: "Indeed. And is that the kind of feeling you are looking for – that kind of positive? Would that feeling bring you peace?"

Jerry: "Yes, it would."

Me: "What do you need to be able to get yourself there?"

Jerry: "I just have to get that business back in shape. I have to start marketing, and I know I need to network more, and…" *[The "shoulds" start pouring out. And his soft, bright energy drops to the floor.]*

Me: "… And you will. I can hear you are ready to go to work. And I hear you believe work can't be anything but WORK. Is that true?"

Jerry: "Yep. Or at least that's how it's always seemed until now."

Me: "You know, you can change that."

Despite his exhaustion, his business was the determining factor for his "happy ending." Meanwhile, despite the awareness of his true passions and spiritual sense of self, he remained locked in thinking patterns that prevented him from moving forward. I suspected the lack of balance in his life further complicated his stress within the business.

As our first session closed, I could hear two agendas:

1. **Jerry's external goal** related to what he needed to do to create financial security. For him, that was to rev up his business, get more clients, raise his prices, and similar practices that cultivate profitability.

2. **Jerry's inner goal** to discover that "next thing" – something that would bring happiness and joy into his life. This was reflected in his sidebar comments about romance, retirement and the great outdoors.

There was a clear split between what Jerry wanted and what he thought he should be focused on and do. He was locked in a polarity, unable to see that his options weren't just black and white. It was even more evident that he was going to put up a good defense as to why one couldn't happen without the other. He left this session armed with ten action items related to marketing his business.

Whole Person Coaching is a powerful process for anyone wanting to create holistic, positive and sustainable change. In short, we've found an unparalleled level of human development and personal success through a reliance on the unified perspectives and wisdom of head-based intellect, heart-based values, and passion and gut-based instincts. As we just saw in Jerry's case, we can't ignore a sense of spiritual or social knowing as well. This process is usually accomplished by tapping into the wisdom of these multiple intelligences through powerful questions and reflection. But when we are out of alignment, we only listen to select parts of ourselves. And like one piece of a larger puzzle, it doesn't give us the whole picture.

Jerry's head was shouldering all the weight, trapping him in the forbidding restraints of his rational mind. His devotion to fitness and physical motion helped relieve some of the stress of being intellectually stuck and potentially overextended. But that wasn't enough. My hope was that, by helping him reconnect to his whole self, he could step away from the outdated perspective as to what was possible for him.

In the sessions that followed, the challenge became where to focus his attention. The great divide was between his head and his heart: building a business he didn't really love or trying to discover what would *really* be most fulfilling for him in the long-run. One week, he focused on the business, the marketing and sales tactics (a.k.a. 'the grind'). The next week, he would give himself permission to focus on exploring new potentials for his future. He even explored becoming a teacher, or potentially spending a year in the mountains. But more often than not, he also continued to dance in fear and doubt, never taking action toward marketing his business at the level he needed to see results.

When the time is right, we can see

Jerry's diverse career path embodied a range of experience. As he worked toward his goals to build his business, he'd share his capacity to competently advise people on everything from farming techniques and wilderness maintenance to high-end remodeling construction, home inspections, and even matters of spirituality. Yet despite this nearly bottomless well of expertise, he'd fall back on what he felt were practical steps to build his business.

Me: "Jerry – we've been working on your business for the past few weeks. How are you feeling about your results?"

Jerry: "It's a lot of work. Almost never-ending. And I'm just feeling so tired all the time. I've even cancelled some of my bike rides. I'm just exhausted. I go home after my inspections and my body just aches… Something has to stop."

Me: "What do you feel has to stop? But wait! Before you answer. I'd like to try something. Remember your trail story and how happy you felt? Where did you feel that?"

Jerry: "I felt it in my body. You remember that."

Me: "So if you were to take a deep breath followed by a full exhale, what might your body say about what has to stop?" *[I gesture for him to put his hand on his belly.]*

Jerry: "My thoughts are pretty negative. I know better."

Me: "Are you referring to the Critic inside your mind?"

Jerry: "Yes, it's always in full stereo."

Me: "How can you turn it off?"

Jerry: "You can turn off the voice of reason? I mean that nasty critic? Boy you could make millions if you could bottle that one up." *[Laughs at himself.]*

Me: "Yes, you can. And I appreciate your vote of confidence – I can raise my rates if it helps…"

The white noise of life can make decisions difficult, even impossible. But Whole Person Coaching cuts through mental and emotional chaos, quickly and permanently. The adage about 'the forest through the trees' is a very real struggle for many of us. Mired in our own rational modes of thinking, we fall victim to the common-sense reasoning of our own minds, not to mention the expectations of others. These stumbling blocks throw the door wide open for doubt to infiltrate our confidence. And once it takes hold, it can often keep us stuck and struggling for years.

Back to Jerry…

Me: "Here's the challenge: you've been pushing hard for the past few weeks, and you've accomplished a lot. Would you be open to doing something for yourself? And I mean something just for you that doesn't include your business?"

Jerry: "I could sign up for the European Cross-Country Ski Race. But I'm not in shape and it's only three months away. I'd have to get airfare, and that costs a lot of money, and I don't know anyone..."

Me: [*gently interrupting the old story*] "Yes, I can hear your critic loud and clear, and to be honest it's really powerful today. That being said, you are highly resourceful. Inside of your life-tales, you've proven to me that it will be just a matter of minutes before you solve these details. Seriously, can I challenge you? I've heard you dance back and forth between your business and creating your next life chapter. You've run circles around most people with your business. You're accomplished in that aspect of your life. But what about the rest of your life?"

Jerry had achieved more than most entrepreneurs during our coaching sessions. He was obviously well on his way to making the money he felt he needed. He even raised his rates and gave himself days off. But it still wasn't enough for him to feel financially secure.

In disgust, Jerry said to me: "I know. I know. I'll explore it. I actually have been." [*He opens his briefcase to show me printouts from various websites.*]

Me: "Wow! You're holding out on me! Should I give you my P.O. Box for the postcard?"

Jerry: "You're too funny."

Me: "I wasn't joking."

Magic of the moment

I wasn't sure if what just happened was going to make a difference. But within this session, things felt different. As we headed into our last few sessions, I had to trust in the process and hold faith he would find his way to the peace and security he sought.

A few months later, I got that postcard. It was simple yet moving: it depicted a big yellow happy face. I smiled from head to toe. Jerry entered not one but two races, both of which culminated in the adventure of a lifetime, as well as opportunities to make new friends from afar.

Happily, ever after

Jerry stopped by my office a month later for his final session. He told the great tale of his adventure. His body lifted from the ground and his spirit soared. For the first time, there was no critic in his head! He was online, getting back into the dating scene, and had even been on a few dates already. His magnetic personality was surely going to receive some success. And with his heart filled with positivity and self-trust, he shared some of his insights.

During a closing session in Whole Person Coaching, we travel back in time and celebrate our client's track record and successes. In doing so, we help them see that the work accomplished is now something they hold forever. The skills and lessons learned are now part of their DNA – readily available for times in the future when they might get stuck. We refer to this quality, transferred from the coaching process, as "self-innovation." In short, it's one's ability to develop their own inner coach and includes all the benefits that come with being more self-aware and proactive in one's life.

In our final session, I asked Jerry: "What have you learned about yourself as a result of your work in coaching?"

Jerry: "You know, when we first spoke, I was at a point where I really needed a change. It was time to give up my business and do something else. Deep down, that's not only what I wanted but also what I needed. I'd ridden the horse to the end and needed to get on another horse. But I just couldn't see any options. I wanted more money. I wanted to get more clients and facilitate my retirement by making the business more salable. And I realize now, in the process of working though that, I was just plain physically tired and emotionally spent. The logic of my head was the only thing I could hear or trust. Now I know better than to listen only to my intellectual self."

Me: "Are you speaking about the amazing dance you performed between your heart, gut and mind?"

Jerry: *[laughing]* "Exactly. My heart says, 'go have fun', but my mind says, 'you only have one chance here'. That message kept me awake. Literally, going, going, going. Insanely going. Of course, that's why I was always so great as a self-employed person. I needed that fear to motivate me. It got me this far."

Me: "And… do you still need that fear?"

Jerry: "A little fear is always good. It keeps you moving. But balance in life is also necessary. Life can be good, but not when it's one-sided. I'm able to see the necessity for balance now. I can feel the difference in my body and in my mind. I'm peaceful."

Me: "OK, Jerry, in the name of self-coaching, what advice do you have for your future self?"

Jerry: "I would tell my future self to get a life! Work to play."

Me: "That's awesome. You've upped your rates. You're making the same amount of money while working less hours. You are on the trails and roads more than ever, and even back in the dating scene. What do you have planned for your next trip?"

Jerry: "Ah yes, I have done a lot. And that next trip…" *[He starts listing his many options.]* "This time next year, I'm going to be retired. I'm going to be out of this business. I may even be on a cross-country bicycling trip."

Me: "Like I said, I love those postcards!"

As we said goodbye, I knew I was going to miss this guy. His work, commitment and devotion to learning were inspiring. Despite his initial fear, he was then and remains today an easily likeable guy who is poised to change the world. The icing on the cake is that a year later Jerry was informed by his CPA that he's got the green light to retire.

Jerry's story is not unlike the thousands of Whole Person Coaching clients who are locked in habitual patterns, unknowingly sabotaging their success. Working with the whole person, you can offer alternative ways to connect to and integrate their whole being. Your efforts can empower others to create life happiness, balance and fulfillment while providing the skills and tools to maintain these changes far into the future.

That truth brings us to our last case study.

Meet Jackie: from invisible to invincible

I had a corporate coaching client last spring we'll call "Jackie" for confidentiality purposes. Jackie hired me to help develop her public-speaking ability. Driven to panic attacks and even tears with the threat of public speaking, she'd endured years of stressful presentations that were unrepresentative of her abilities due to her overwhelming nervousness. Similarly, she'd remained stuck in the same position due to a fear of failure and conflict. This despite numerous offers for advancement that included greater responsibility, more visibility and influence, and a higher salary.

It's important to understand that, her fears notwithstanding, Jackie was highly productive within her own little arena. As team leader, she'd led her group to become one of the highest performing departments in the company – a level of mastery and success she attributed to being open and authentic with her team.

Due to her effective communication skills, something else was happening she hadn't intended. Jackie's team and it's communicative, effective performance had gained the attention of her company's senior leaders. She'd been asked by the president of the company to share her team's secret to success at an awards dinner… in front of the entire company… in six weeks.

Realizing she needed help, Jackie sought me out after hearing about my work through other departmental leaders and management-level peers in her office.

Jackie's initial goal was to write a thought-provoking, educational speech that would bring laughter and learning to the room. She loved humor. Her secondary goal – as she referred to her little "secret" – was to abolish her nervousness when speaking in front of others.

But here's the thing: Jackie was smart, savvy and knew exactly what she wanted. She just had to know where to look, and how to interpret what she saw there.

During our initial meetings, Jackie shared her struggles. Typical of most of us who've created a false story around the experience of public speaking, her imagined experience reflected her unsettled state. To be fair, public speaking is the second most common fear, beat out only by our fear of heights. And in some polls, public speaking (a.k.a. "public sweating") firmly holds the top spot.

Jackie was deeply concerned with how well she'd do, how others might perceive her, and what impact it might have on her future at the company. Occasionally, I'd hear a softer voice of reason, one that offered the insight that all her perceptions might not actually be true. But her primary story was filled with fear and conflicting thoughts – a recipe for unrelenting stress and sleepless nights that nearly drove her crazy.

With less than two months to prepare, she had a lot to do and little time to do it in. But she also had five business trips before her big day, five opportunities to practice her speaking and work up to the main event.

Because of its universal nature, Whole Person Coaching is applicable to any aspect of an individual's life – personal or professional. Better yet, the learning and development that occur from the change-making process in one area of an individual's life can be applied to other areas as well. This gives you the potential to transform an entire life, one story at a time. In fact, it's not uncommon to witness a client creating changes in alternative areas of their life then build the confidence and competence required to tackle the larger and seemingly more difficult ones.

Jackie's game-changing conversation happened on our fifth session. I asked her to step into a preferred future related to her presentation. Specifically, I challenged her to author the most powerful story imaginable about giving a speech for her company's awards dinner.

As she began to describe that future moment, she painted a bleak and treacherous outcome, creating an emotional backdrop that triggered her into a deep sweat (literally). I could immediately hear the tension in her voice and see it overtake her body as she fell into a worst-case future that had not yet been created.

Shortly into her tailspin, I gently interrupted her:

Me: "Jackie, that's a powerful tale. But I was inviting you to step into your most powerful self, the part of you that shines in the public light."

[I remind her of another story she had shared related to a recent experience performing karaoke with friends.]

Me: "Jackie, consider how you were on stage with your peers at Songbox Karaoke bar. Who was that rock star?"

Jackie: *[Laughing and melting with relief.]* "That was the fun part of me. Public speaking is just not fun."

Me: "I can tell you believe it isn't fun. But what if it was? Imagine yourself on stage. You're speaking in public. And you're having fun." *[I wait patiently for her response.]*

Jackie: *[Closes her eyes and then quickly grows frustrated with the process.]* "I'm struggling to do this."

Me: "Would it be helpful if I walked you through a visualization?"

Jackie: "Yes, it would."

Me: "Ok when you are ready, I'd like you to take a slow deep breath and then an even longer exhale." *[We breathe together.]* "Now a few more deeper breaths, taking the time you need to just drop in and find yourself in a relaxed space. *[I pause and watch her face and body melt into a more restful state.]*

"Now, I'd like you to imagine you are traveling down a forest path, one that is special – just for you. At the end of this path, you find yourself at a familiar place. Maybe this place is by the ocean, a lake, a river, a meadow. Where you're standing in this moment, it's somewhere you feel at ease and comfortable within. *[Jackie's shoulders drop.]* In this special place, I want you to imagine you are sitting in front of an audience. But not just any audience, a group of people that are excited to hear from you. People who want you to succeed at getting your message out. Now, at the front of that audience, there are two of your coworkers, the ones who know you well. The two you trust most. Go ahead and see them there, looking at you, and feel the support they have to offer. If they have spoken wisdom for you, take it in. Perhaps it's just their confident smiles or gestures of encouragement.

Now embody the support of the rest of your audience. They are there just for you. They want to hear your secrets and learn something from you." *[Jackie twitches and jostles her body.]* "Inside this safe place and with these supportive people, how does it feel to just be there with them? Take notice of how you're feeling in your body at this moment. Stay with that sensation wherever it arises and until it passes." *[She appears to have drifted inside. I hold space for her to get in touch with her bodily sensations.]* "Whatever arises is perfectly OK. Whether it's a thought, feeling or bodily sensation. Let it flow. Find yourself grounded in the support your audience and peers have to offer you. Feel their kind, loving appreciation for you and all you do."

[I remain silent. The curling of Jackie's lips indicates something has arrived in that clever mind of hers. She bursts out laughing and begins to share.]

Jackie: "You're going to think I'm crazy, but it sure would be fun if this speech wasn't just me on stage, but my whole team. We could put together a play of sorts and collaboratively speak about how and why our team is the way it is."

Me: "You mean the top team in the company?"

Jackie: "Yes! We are a top team because of the fun we have together and the collaborative approach reflected in our motto: 'We are all on top. So, who's on first?'"

Me: "That's a clever motto – I'm excited. What else?"

Jackie: "Do you think this'll fly? After all, the president of the company wanted me to speak..." *[A look of concern crosses her face.]*

Me: "What do you think?"

Jackie: "I'm gonna ask. I think it would be a wonderful way to represent myself and the team. I can't imagine him saying no, especially if this process informs others on how *we* do it: together."

Me: "Splendid. It sounds like you are going to model what your team does on stage. That's a great idea. How are you feeling about this possibility right now?"

Jackie: "On fire! And look – I'm not sweating."

Me: "Great! I can already see you there..." *[I gesture to a crowd enthusiastically applauding and smile with anticipation.]*

Jackie: "I am *so* there! I can't wait to go to work tomorrow."

Me: "That must feel good. Anything else for today?"

Jackie: "I feel complete." *[She grabs her stuff and jets out the door with a skip in her walk.]*

After receiving immediate and unreserved approval from her boss (with a hint of what Jackie would later realize was also trust), the evening finally arrived. When the dinner plates had been cleared and the cake and coffee served, Jackie and her team took the stage. As a group, they'd stayed after work late into the night for nearly two weeks. They'd written a humorous play that told a story of the magical power of collaboration and what they'd dubbed "the team play."

Within the skit, each member had a limelight moment. Then it was Jackie's turn. Without missing a beat, several of the team members unveiled a karaoke machine and accompanied her in the background as she performed a cover of "Roar" by Katy Perry. Jackie and her team received standing applause from the whole company. The following Monday, the company president invited Jackie to his office to discuss the evening. And by discuss, I mean pick her brain. Jackie was offered a new position in the company within which she was responsible for developing other teams, both locally and internationally! Further, the company president understood and admired her desire to continue working on her fear of public speaking. He had no doubt her ongoing development would enable her to lead the company into even better customer service. As a result, he offered a stipend to further her additional coaching!

During Jackie's final coaching session, I learned another of her secret wishes had been granted. To celebrate her promotion, she'd gathered a few friends and visited her favorite karaoke bar. That night, as she walked off stage, she was met eye-to-eye with a man who had been curious about the charming, confident woman he saw on stage. They had begun a slow, but promising romance.

Working through her fear of public speaking gave Jackie the additional confidence to reinvent her story in other aspects of her life – in this case: romance.

The secret behind Jackie's success...

When Jackie first came to be coached, the depth of her fears had consumed her. This state dramatically impacted not only this aspect of her life but the rest of it as well. As a result, she was paralyzed by her anxiousness and didn't feel resourced enough to take the action needed for success.

Through the Whole Person Coaching process, we identified that, even though she was nervous speaking in front of an audience, Jackie had confidence in abundance while on stage performing karaoke. By leveraging her experience and confidence singing, she found within herself the courage to speak. And by drawing upon the story of who she was in each situation, she was able to quickly rewrite the story of herself as a speaker by envisioning the best possible outcome – one that was an accurate reflection of her abilities and talents. But it wasn't until we worked through her emotional discomfort and fears, leveraging mindfulness meditations to help her through the physical sensations that had once sent her into a sweat-soaked tailspin, that she truly broke free. She found her own resourcefulness through our creative approach. And it allowed her to step into her innate power and personal best.

As a Whole Person Coach, you will work with your clients on many levels. You'll attend to everything from their core experiences to their beliefs and innermost needs. You will work with the interconnected nature of thoughts, feelings and bodily sensations. In particular, you'll be tuned in to how these three aspects of an individual interact to form the story they are living in. For Jackie, her phobia of public speaking produced a state of deep discomfort. This further propelled her into forecasting worst-case possible outcomes. Although she had previously employed numerous strategies and actions to write the perfect speech, it wasn't enough. The key to her success was attending to her mind state and to find the inner peace and confidence she needed to shine.

Master you: master coaching

The stories we've looked at in this chapter represent only the beginning of what you can achieve. Whole Person Coaching (WPC) offers a universal system that works at the speed and depth necessary to facilitate positive, sustainable change in a wide variety of applications. These range from day-to-day conversations, relationships and businesses to building leaders and creating change on a global scale.

Whole Person Coaching is one of the most comprehensive and effective ways to work with others. The tools and techniques of this method are universally applicable to any client or organization. Alex, Jerry and Jackie's stories, although unique to their individual circumstances, speak to the power of addressing the whole person. More significantly, they offer evidence of WPC's extraordinary results, supporting individuals to be self-innovating in all aspects of their life, and for the rest of their life.

The coach as an instrument of change

Your ability to shift and adapt your approach, elegantly advancing your ideal clients beyond even their most feared stopping blocks, is what makes you highly desirable to those who need you. It's also what puts you on the radar for top-paying clients who have not achieved the success they've been working toward with other coaches in the past.

As a Whole Person Coach, the creative process you offer elevates the coaching conversation, the work and the results. The coaching conversation co-evolves between the interactions of coach and client, with the end goal of each session being to leave the client feeling empowered, fully resourceful and able to listen and respond at their very best. Your ability to recognize what is needed in the present moment improves the effectiveness of this process. It also closes the gap between where your client currently stands and where they want to be.

From the outside, much of coach training looks as though you develop your skills to help others. And ultimately, that's true. But many of the most impressive coaches have done their own work too. They've allowed coaching and their training process to transform their own lives. Offering tools and techniques designed specifically for a process of self-mastery, coaching has opened their minds and made them even more effective at seeing within. For some, this takes shape in becoming deeply present and attuned to their own needs. Others discover the ability to truly step into their own fullest expression and truest nature. And for all of us, it's about recognizing the way in which our presence affects others. Not only do your own relationship and communication skills excel in all areas of your life, they also create a profound shift in the way in which you go through the world and interact with everyone around you: clients, coworkers, friends and family. In Whole Person Coaching, we have a saying: the person you are being in the moment is the one who is creating your future.

At Coach Training World, we believe coaching is a skill set that should be possessed by everyone and anyone looking to be highly effective in all aspects of their life – regardless of application. In many ways, coaching is a lifestyle choice, a way of relating to yourself, others and the world in meaningful and powerful ways. It's a communication style that moves beyond the negativity and what's not working to uncover solutions and open-hearted conversations. It is also a process that can help anyone get unstuck and back into flow in any situation.

Chapter review and coming attractions

Whole Person Coaching is an accelerated learning and development process in which game-changing conversations, often lasting only minutes, have resounding effects on clients. As a trusted process of coaches across the globe, Whole Person Coaching is revolutionizing the way coaches and clients alike access their own innate wisdom of the whole self and step into their wholeness.

Next Up: The expert holistic coaching skills and capacity of Whole Person Coaching allow you to specialize in your chosen area of interest or population. So we'll take a closer look at the most popular niches and discover which is best suited to you and how to further customize within. From a practical point of view, I'm also going to show you how other coaches are currently applying WPC to a wide variety of contexts and client bases.

~ *In Your Journal* ~

Reflect on a past time in which you "wrote" the ending of a future experience in your imagination before you stepped a single foot into the moment.

- Was the ending you thought of positive or otherwise?

- How were you feeling physically and emotionally as a result of the story you were telling yourself?

- What do you think motivated this perspective?

- Write down how you feel when you think about the worst-case scenario for something that hasn't happened.

- Does it come easy? Is this a standard story for you?

- Now write down what might be possible if you imagined the best possible outcome... with absolutely no limitations!

~5~

Uniquely You: Specialize in your ideal niche

There is no better way to create a meaningful career or business than to build from your deepest passions and potential – guided by your soul's calling.

As a trained Whole Person Coach, your expert holistic coaching skills and capacity to affect sustainable change by working with the whole person allow you to specialize in your chosen area of interest or population.

For this reason, Whole Person coaches run the gamut from life, wellness, mindfulness, empowerment and relationship coaches to business, spiritual, nonprofit and leadership coaches. And that's naming just a few. In the same way, you too can be positioned to work in a wide variety of coaching contexts, whether you opt to focus on one dedicated niche or decide to serve a diverse variety of clients.

Be true to you

Being true to who you are as a whole person and leveraging your individual qualities is a vital step in the pursuit of happiness. It's also an essential element if you want to make your difference in the world, and prosper by doing so.

Many coaches start coach training with their end goal in mind. Like physical therapy team Kelly and Martin, who you met in Chapter 1. They wanted to help their existing client base in more profound ways. Or Christina, whose experience in a challenging divorce brought her to the realization she could help others avoid the same painful mistakes. In the same way, you too might have an ideal population you'd love to serve.

But this isn't always the case. Many people discover their ideal niche through the coach training process. Here you are exposed to a diverse variety of clients and coaching contexts. Your firsthand experience working with others provides the opportunity to consciously choose a type of coaching and specialize in a niche uniquely suited to your greatest strengths and deepest passions. Rightfully so. Your path to a career, business and life you truly love is as unique as those you will one day serve.

Inside this chapter, we'll explore the most popular types of coaching and dive deep into the numerous opportunities within each category for specializing within your preferred niche. We'll also view these options through the real-life lens of our graduates and their inspirational stories.

The choice is yours

There are virtually no boundaries for reinventing or leveling up your work with Whole Person Coaching. That's a claim few people in any industry can make. The manner and arena in which you employ coaching's tools and methodologies will vary based on your personal or professional area of interest.

The most popular types of coaching include:

- Life Coaching
- Health & Wellness Coaching
- Career Coaching
- Small Business / Startup / Entrepreneur Coaching
- Executive Coaching
- Team Coaching
- Spiritual Coaching
- Relationship Coaching

Each type offers its own challenges and rewards. Based on your experience and individuality, some will be better suited to you than others. For example, if you spent the last twenty years working in the corporate arena (and loving it there), executive or leadership coaching may be a natural fit. On the other hand, if you're looking to transition out of a corporate career while leveraging your love of whole foods and nutrition, becoming a health and fitness coach might be ideal for you. And becoming a life coach could be your next move, especially if you love working with a wide variety of topics and major life transitions.

Where do you see yourself fitting into the following options?

Life Coaching

One of the perks of being a life coach is you are guaranteed a lot of variety, not to mention the endless ways you can support others. As a life coach, you focus on numerous aspects of your client's life, evidenced by a coaching plan that covers everything from their career, business and identity to health, enjoyment, creativity, spirituality and even relationships. This is true whether their end goals pertain to creating life balance, achieving personal fulfillment, life transitions, or working toward some aspect of success.

The key to successful life coaching is to focus on your clients' "whole" lives as interconnected. This multi-dimensional approach is what improves their overall level of happiness, success and prosperity. It is also what enables them to transform multiple aspects of their lives for the better.

A common path among life coaches is to work with clients who are currently traveling a path similar to the coach's past experiences. For example, perhaps you've reinvented your life after an unexpected job-loss that sent you on a year-long self-exploration, traveling around the world. Now you want to help others find their joy as well. Or maybe you are a successful entrepreneur who has created a life of balance and ease through mindfulness and yoga. Now you want to capitalize on your knowledge and experience while giving the next generation a helping hand. So you focus on the business owner's whole life and create a service package that makes that the central component of a sustainable business.

Regardless of the origin of your experience, it can be leveraged to effectively guide the coaching process. Your clients take great comfort in the fact that they're championed by a kindred spirit – someone who has successfully traveled a similar path.

A further subset of this niche is seen in those who customize their life coaching services with a focus on anything from work-life balance, intimate relationships, and creative expression to life purpose and meaning. Recently, I've also noticed a surge in life coaches who specialize in mindfulness, energy healing and spirituality. The beauty of life coaching is it's virtually limitless in how you serve others.

Life coaching is also the perfect pairing if you are already serving a client base. In this case, you simply add the tools and methodology of coaching into your existing business. Those who successfully incorporate life coaching into their existing practice often include:

- Personal Trainers
- Nutritionists
- Social Workers
- Mindfulness Practitioners
- Yogis

- Energy Workers
- Hynotherapists
- Massage Therapists
- Counselors
- And many more…

Who works with a life coach?

As a life coach, your clients typically seek you out as the result of a significant life change or transition. Others may be stuck in the doldrums and recognize the need for change even without a wake-up call. Standing at a crossroads, they are looking for their next steps, seeking clarity, self-understanding, motivation and direction (often in several areas of their life at once). Whether they are looking for a little life tune-up or a complete life reinvention, you can expect their list of goals to vary based on their individual needs.

They may want to simultaneously lose weight, find their ideal partner, start painting and update their résumé. Many are seeking a more meaningful and rewarding life, where others have specific needs in mind. One of the more common requests I've received in recent years, among clients across the spectrum, is a yearning to rediscover and reclaim their wholeness and be more authentic.

Should you specialize as a life coach?

Life coaching is for you if you relish working at the deeper levels of change. If you want to go beyond checking off accountability lists to creating transformational results, or you love working holistically and touching on multiple aspects of a person's life, you'll love life coaching.

Becoming a life coach can be especially appealing if your own life pursuits have you jumping from job to job or struggling to make your college degree truly serve you. It might be time for you to align your life's passion and purpose. And there is no better way. By focusing on life coaching, you'll not only be adding rich value to your résumé and future potential as an employee or business owner, you are also guaranteed to tune up your own life along the way. That's why many a coach will tell you they first came to coach training for their own benefit.

A focus on life coaching isn't just for coaches either. It's for anyone who wants to help their special people thrive in the possibilities life has to offer, including teachers, parents and caregivers.

As we explore the remaining popular categories, you'll notice that each centers on one or two aspects of a person's life. These options are indeed more focused and, as you'll soon see, are often chosen by those seeking to incorporate specific academic, work-related or other specialized knowledge into their coaching practice.

Meet Sharon Roemmel

Since college, Sharon has worked in some type of helping profession. She's been a social worker, counselor, trainer, massage therapist, teacher at a massage school, and a yoga instructor. Before becoming a coach, she was also a self-employed massage and yoga teacher for almost twenty years and taught part-time at a massage school for nearly six years.

Sharon has spent her life amassing a wide range of skills and experience – all of them in service to others. But she began to notice a need for support around the issue of living a life of purpose in a way that didn't leave people feeling like a casualty. Time and again, she'd watch her students, colleagues, and clients get excited about a path for their lives. But then they'd get stuck, overwhelmed, start to question whether they deserve it, or get beat down in some other way. All too often, these people with big dreams returned to jobs they hated because they couldn't figure out how to make their dream a reality.

"I kept saying, 'someone needs to offer this kind of support'," Sharon says. "Eventually, I realized it was my job."

After graduating from Coach Training World in 2014, Sharon successfully combined her healing and yoga backgrounds with the tools and techniques of professional coaching. It's not uncommon for her to use powerful coaching questions, breath work, energy work, and body awareness… all in a single session.

Sharon specializes in helping women who feel stuck and overwhelmed connect with their purpose and reclaim their vitality and joy. She helps them find clarity about what they want then accompanies them as they discover how to attain it. Whether that dream is running a business, writing a book, or changing jobs, Sharon helps her clients work more consistently on their self-care and places their passions front and center.

"It goes back to the analogy of teaching someone to fish versus giving them a fish," she says. "With Whole Person Coaching, I'm helping my clients get unstuck and do things they've dreamed about for years. But I'm not just helping them get unstuck in the moment. They walk away with awareness and tools that help them in the future."

Today Sharon works with women individually in sessions that span at least three months. In addition to standard coaching sessions, she also leads a range of fun, inspiring personalized retreats, including international retreats, local Oregon weekends, and individual retreats, virtually and in-person. Not surprisingly, she is currently working on a book about retreats.

"I love the flexibility that coaching allows me as a professional," Sharon says. "I can offer coaching at my physical office, on private retreat, via phone or video chat. Plus, coaching enhances the other services I offer – like yoga retreats and teaching – providing my clients faster, more consistent results."

Health & Wellness Coaching

In contrast to a life coach who focuses up-front on goals related to all aspects of a client's life, a health and wellness coach centers on the lifestyle changes that are directly related to a client's health and well-being, taking the whole person into consideration.

As a health and wellness coach, you champion your clients to make conscious lifestyle choices and actions that align with their desired well-being goals. This often means you assist them:

- Create and maintain an exercise program
- Incorporate healthier eating habits
- Promote stress reduction and relaxation
- Eliminate habits of self-sabotage
- Develop a spiritual or emotional mindfulness practice for mind/body well-being

Specialized coaching applications within this niche also commonly involve coping tools and strategies for chronic diseases or adapting to specialized diets. These can include arthritis and other forms of pain caused by inflammation, autoimmune conditions, cancer, and unique concentrations that are often grounded in your personal and professional experience as a coach.

Who works with a health & wellness coach?

As a health & wellness coach, clients seek your help when they are unable to achieve their goals alone or are confronted by a chronic or sudden illness. Recognizing that self-care has fallen to last on their priority list, they're looking for accountability and a non-judgmental partner who motivates them to take better care of themselves.

Although health & wellness coaching clients can be focused on overcoming procrastination and other challenges associated with their health, they may also seek clarity, life-balance, healing strategies and preventative measures. Similar to life coaches, health & wellness coaches want to get to the core of their client's challenges and work at unconscious levels to create sustainable change in their total well-being.

Should you specialize as a health & wellness coach?

Yes, if you enjoy working with the whole person while leveraging your specialized knowledge and experience in the health and well-being arena. While you may focus primarily on your client's physical health, you should also expect to touch on other areas of their life as well. After all, symptoms are never the root of the problem.

Within this branch of coaching, you are typically expected to possess additional knowledge and skills devoted to your client's unique challenges. These skills typically stem from past experience in related workplace fields, academic studies or your own personal health and wellness journey. As a highly supportive health partner, you help clients make choices that honor who they are and their unique health needs, as well as their desired outcomes. Your mission is to keep people on track for living and feeling their best regardless of their current health and wellness status.

Enhancing the services of medical professionals

In recent years, health & wellness coaching has proliferated inside holistic medical and healthcare practices. This accounts for a noticeable rise in the number of doctors, dentists and other alternative healthcare specialists who have recently supplemented their services through partnerships with coaches.

Having a coach on the team enhances their medical expertise with a powerful means of support, accountability and long-term success. In particular, it empowers the client to implement directives or advice put forth by a doctor or professional healthcare advisor. Working with a coach, patients have more "buy-in." In turn, this frequently results in a greater success rate for some forms of treatment and improves states of health overall.

Meet Teresa Rodden

Teresa is a true warrior. She has fought major battles throughout her life... and won them all. Her story is unique in that she embodies the core qualities of a true coach: someone who tirelessly works on herself then uses that knowledge and experience to lift others who struggle on a similar path.

After extricating herself from an abusive relationship – one in which she had become dependent on alcohol to numb her pain – Teresa began to take her first steps toward a new life. In this new version of herself, she was in charge and authentically living.

She came into coaching while working for a weight loss company where she felt limited in her ability to truly help others alter their relationship with food, a coping vice. It was a pattern she was all too familiar with. Though nutrition plays a role in overall health, Teresa realized the drive for change had to come from within. Despite her success in sales with this company, she began to grow restless and frustrated watching the same cycle repeat itself with every client: a short burst of success followed by relapses into previous patterns, and potentially even worse.

So her challenge became to find a system that would facilitate sustainable, lasting improvements for an individual's health and wellness goals. At the same, it would also need to support the varied experiences of each individual and recognize their goals as they sought to overcome alcohol dependency. There were many options available, but few that met her criteria.

"Every program I researched to become a professional in the recovery industry required me to believe and think what's commonly held as truth," Teresa says. "Through my experience, I knew what was told and taught as gospel was not absolute."

It was then that Teresa discovered Whole Person Coaching. She immediately recognized it as a way to provide her clients with a process that could help anyone with change, yet was personalized to each individual. She committed herself to the training to further boost her capabilities and give her clients the reassurance that comes with professional certification. Before long, she had created a successful platform out of her passions.

Today Teresa empowers women who struggle with alcohol and want to change. This includes everyone from lonely stay-at-home moms who find entertainment through wine clubs to top executives who need to shut down their racing thoughts with a brandy or two. Whatever path a woman is on, Teresa can help her retake charge of her life and live sober without struggle.

As a successful solopreneur, Teresa uses her company, Pink Cloud Coaching, to give women the power of choice that – up to this point – they have never received. By applying this power to a woman's WHOLE life, Teresa facilitates the realization that a woman no longer needs to distract herself with alcohol and other self-defeating coping behaviors.

> *"Pink Cloud Coaching is changing the landscape of recovery by offering an interception for women who want to change their relationship with alcohol," she says. "No longer do they have to exit through the one and only door and assume the lifetime identity—alcoholic."*

In addition to coaching sessions, Teresa is the author, of *Wholly Sober*. A highly personal account of her life with alcohol, the book's core message directly represents her services: there is more than one way to live sober. She is also currently at work on additional support materials including talks, workshops, and a workbook for *Wholly Sober*.

Career Coaching

Career coaches are in the enviable position of guiding people into meaningful, rewarding work. This new direction may already align within their wheelhouse or be something entirely new. As a career coach, you foster greater self-understanding and insight for those seeking to discover their ideal professional pursuit or role within an organization or industry.

Typically, those pursuing career coaching fall into one of two focal areas:

- Career advancement
- Career transitions

With career advancement, you routinely focus on developing clients (or in-house employees if you're an internal coach) to assume roles of greater influence and responsibility in the workplace or their industry.

Alternatively, when you work with those at the point of career transition, you find people who are at a crossroads and ready to transition into work that builds on their existing skills. They may also be looking for a track that is more meaningful and challenging.

Regardless of the specific branch of career coaching you opt to focus on, you help your clients self-discover the intersection of their skills, passions, interests and experience. As a result, they become clear on what they truly want and successfully step forward into work that aligns with their greatest strengths and assets.

Who works with a career coach?

If you pursue this path, you'll likely encounter clients who are in the middle of or anticipating career transition. Within this stressful state of change, you assist them to confidently step into their fullest potential, addressing any emotional impacts or limiting beliefs that may be hindering their process.

Your clients desire a trusted confidant, someone who can offer them a safe place to explore. Within this partnership, you champion them towards their very best by enabling them to pursue careers reflective of their true and authentic self – not to mention their unique talents and gifts.

Many people think all they need to land their dream job is a professional-looking résumé. Not so. Add to that the fact that the job search itself can be highly stressful in several ways (and often well before the interviews start). This results in elevated levels of anxiety that lead to feelings of doubt or frustration.

Your job as coach is to help people work through these challenging moments so they effectively represent their true value to current and prospective employers or transition into work they'll absolutely love. You may even help them explore related opportunities within a different company or industry.

Should you specialize as a career coach?

Perhaps you've worked inside a government, academic or corporate environment, helping others with their career moves, and are ready to step out on your own. Or you've lived the risks of leaping around in the corporate arena, expanding your job description to better suit your very best. Now you'd like to coach others to do the same. Career coaching may be a perfect fit for you.

As a career coach, you are interested in matching more than just skills when it comes to careers and jobs. You value the freedom to explore and discover the job that aligns with the passion, skills and career path that is true to your clients' genuine needs and interests.

Often this is related to helping people self-discover how they can find work that allows them to bring their whole self to the table. Your wisdom is the tipping point others need to break free from their current perceived constraints and the cycles of doubt and limitation keeping them stuck in fields they don't enjoy or may not be suited for. Your encouragements help them stay true to their deepest callings and find work they truly can't wait to get to as they jump out of bed in the morning.

Many coaches find career coaching to be highly rewarding, not only for the help it provides others, but also for the immediacy of the results. Your clients find work and enjoy promotions and greater levels of personal and professional success, often in just a few short weeks or months. They also overcome fear and resistance through increased confidence, and achieve improvements in creativity, innovation and overall performance. These personal "bests" aid them not only in their professional lives, but in their personal lives as well.

Meet Claire Yeung

Before training to become a professional coach, Claire had been a successful attorney for twenty-three years. Despite a six-figure salary and the respect and status she'd earned in more than two decades, she was unhappy. Claire was overworked and burned out. Even worse, she was forced to keep up a "happy" façade for clients and coworkers – a practice that eventually caused her to vent her irritability toward loved ones and friends.

Her health was the next to suffer. In 2012, she contracted a mysterious virus that lasted for six months and made her feel like "the walking dead." Claire had come to a point where, in order to move forward, she knew she had to reevaluate her life. That's when she realized: there was a kinder person inside of her, dying to get out.

> *"Becoming a coach has allowed me to find my purpose in life: to help others live their best lives," Claire says. "It has also given me my life back and made me a kinder, less judgmental, more peaceful person. I can now strive to live my life with grace, which I couldn't do before because I was so miserable."*

Embracing both her inner achiever and adventurer, Claire learned to bring forward those parts of her persona in useful ways. She quit her job as an attorney with no plan whatsoever except to get well. Once she recovered her health, she began to investigate the coaching profession, which she'd heard about a few years prior (funny how the meaningful things tend to stick with us!).

Today Claire is all about momentum. She provides one-on-one coaching and workshops for high-achieving professionals that range in focus from career, leadership, and other aspects of business to retirement and family relationships. Claire uses Whole Person coaching skills and techniques to reframe how her clients view their current situation. In doing so, she helps them move past the hurdles that prevent them from achieving what they want.

"Coaching has allowed me to become an entrepreneur doing what I love," she says. "Prior to becoming a coach, I never in my wildest dreams thought I would be able to build a business doing something I was passionate about."

Claire's passions have since taken her to great heights. In addition to coaching sessions, she created a *One Life... No Regrets Weekend*. The focus was to help attendees transform their lives, enabling them to live passionately and purposefully. Her book (*The Eighty-Year Rule: What Would You Regret Not Doing in Your Lifetime?*) and e-course (*Making Every Moment Count*) expand on her theme of moving individuals from where they are currently at in life to where they want to be. Also an accomplished speaker and lecturer, she frequently presents to business groups on the topic of 'Becoming the Hero of Your Own Story' and teaches at the Justice Institute of British Columbia within the Bachelor of Law Enforcement program.

Business Coaching

Coaching for small businesses, startups and entrepreneurs optimizes the potential of a new or existing business by focusing on the company's founder. Serving business owners and entrepreneurs, you enable your clients to sharpen their presence and leadership skills, develop or expand their business, and elevate their people to success. As with health and wellness coaches, a business coach typically has previous knowledge, experience and expertise they are building upon by using coaching to help others.

Your mission is to evaluate your client's present business condition, as well as their role as an influencer within it. From there, you work to help them more readily understand and advance their chosen business agenda. At the same time, you instill within them the tools necessary to become a highly effective leader and business owner in line with their personality and individual strengths.

Who works with a business coach?

As a small business/entrepreneur coach, clients come to you for your ability to champion them to self-discover and create the business they really want. Your clients are seeking to be more effective in their communication, strategic in their decision-making, and want to develop their time and people-management skills.

Depending on your area of experience and expertise, you may also be called upon to help them with everything from marketing and social media to speaking, trade show presentations, and other forms of public address. In the broadest terms, your goal is to enable individuals and their businesses to prosper.

Almost without exception, your clients want to be more self-confident, optimistic and motivated as they create ease and flow in the fast-paced, ever-demanding business environment. Many are also looking for more effective ways to be successful in their business endeavors while maintaining a healthy work-life balance.

The best part of becoming a business coach is that the tools and philosophy associated with your services almost always spill over into your clients' personal lives. Makes sense, doesn't it? If you stop to think about your whole being – mental, emotional, physical, social and spiritual – how many of these five aspects affect your work and vice versa? All of them... and often more than some people would like! So, by considering each of the core elements of a whole person, you immediately extend the benefit you offer your business clients while elevating the scope and value of your services.

Should you specialize as a business coach?

Yes! Especially if you value addressing the needs of the whole company and the deeper dimensions that block an entrepreneur or business owner from truly flourishing.

It's also worth noting this branch of coaching is highly valued in North America. The International Coach Federation recently published the *2016 ICF Global Coaching Study* in which they reported 3,100 business managers and leaders are now using coaching skills within their daily workplace interactions.[1] That number jumps to 10,900 when you take into account business owners and entrepreneurs throughout the world.

Many who become business coaches are already business owners themselves (yours truly among them). This unique experience enables them to support their clients through the full spectrum of business challenges. It typically includes upstarts, business launches, day-to-day operations, business development and growth, and even succession planning.

While certain clients may call upon you to wear several hats, some coaches choose to specialize in a specific subset of this niche. This enhances the value of their services, positioning them above those who opt to provide only standard business coaching. Almost always based on the coach's individual strengths and experience, popular subsets include:

---

1 International Coach Federation. *2016 ICF Global Coaching Study*. Research. Accessed April 4, 2018. https://coachfederation.org/research/global-coaching-study.

- Work-life Balance/Mindfulness
- Product Research and Development
- Speaking for Professionals
- Sales Effectiveness
- Leadership and Communication Skills
- Training and Development
- Family-Owned Businesses
- Speaking/Presentations
- Franchises
- Branding and Marketing
- Digital Marketing
- Content Development and Marketing
- Employee Training and Development

The most successful small business coaches are typically those who have previously laid the tracks of a successful entrepreneurial venture or have direct inside business experience to draw upon. They know the road a business owner must travel and are thus a highly valuable resource. Now they want to give back to the next generation of business owners. For this reason, small business coaches frequently originate from within the corporate arena or their own entrepreneurial ventures. Your experience essentially qualifies you to offer knowledge on a wide variety of topics and considerations encountered in the daily routine of business operation.

But there are exceptions to this rule. If you are someone who possesses generalized knowledge, such as the experience and skills related to a specific need for a new or small business, you can still become an asset in their business success tool kit as their coach. Perhaps you have a degree or advanced training in speaking and communications. Maybe you're highly organized and can prioritize a lengthy to-do list in your sleep. And if you are one of the rare few who have a natural ability to defuse potentially explosive interpersonal situations, you'll find your powers of disarmament have tremendous value in the business arena.

Small business or start-up coaching is for you if you love working at the ground level to help business clients achieve their best while bouncing around a few topics throughout your conversations.

Meet Feroshia Knight

Yes, yours truly has a success story too. Spoiler alert: you're holding a big part of it in your hands! For more than two decades, it has been my mission and privilege to walk side-by-side with coaching clients and students alike, helping them align with their life's greatest aspirations. I couldn't have done it without the highly specialized approach detailed in this book.

> *"Becoming a business coach has enabled me to share my wisdom through a highly collaborative, creative process that places my clients at the center of the work. Like no other profession in the world, this has allowed me to touch lives and companies, inside and out – lifting them up to reshape the world around me. With each individual or business leader who finds their way, making their own impact in the world, my impact grows exponentially!"*

After a successful ten-year run serving top-tier companies, business leaders and entrepreneurs as a global marketing expert, I woke up and realized something was deeply missing. I had my own business. Woo-hoo! But where were the freedom, creativity and purpose that were supposed to go along with it?

With a strong background in sales, marketing, speaking and education, coaching was a no-brainer for me. In fact, it was the only way I could create multiple streams of income by leveraging my brilliance and remaining exactly who I was. In truth: I had to stop, listen to my inherent wisdom, and rediscover who I was. But that's a story for another book (I know, I know: shameless plug).

Long story short, I didn't change careers. But I found a way to improve everything in my existing business by incorporating the tools and methodology of my unique approach: Whole Person Coaching. From there, like so many others who've found their unique niche, I was able to translate my skills as a coach into something that fits me like a glove, finally claiming my own unique niche as the Digital Dollar Diva!

> *"Your life experience and expertise only add to your services as a coach. Where else in the world is that true? Becoming a professional coach allows you to not only use but capitalize on your volumes of experience. In doing so, it gives you a choice. You can change careers entirely, or you can do what you're doing now in a way that's far more meaningful to you and makes your dream life come true."*

Today I wear multiple hats and enjoy the invigorating nature of helping my business-owner and leadership clients prosper from their passions and make the world a better place. By far, becoming a coach was the best decision I've ever made, and I believe it only gets better from here.

Executive Coaching

Top-tier executive leaders frequently struggle to realize their full potential, as well as that of their company or division. They are too inundated by the operational demands and stresses of day-to-day business. Executive coaches fill the void by working with these leaders to self-identify their problem areas then develop the executive-level skills that enable them to positively impact the entire organization.

As an executive coach, you focus on developing highly effective, influential leaders who are currently working within the top rank of the company hierarchy, typically C-level. This frequently encompasses:

- Developing leadership and management skills to more effectively motivate and inspire employees
- Transitioning individuals to a higher level of management or new assignment
- Acting as a sounding board
- Improving communication
- Cultivating time management strategies
- Improving work-life balance
- Assisting with succession planning

Executive coaches are also frequently called upon to encompass aspects of life coaching, wellness coaching and often, effective communication. As an executive coach, you are most effective when working holistically with your clients, leveraging their whole being to achieve optimal, sustainable results in all aspects of their life.

Who works with an executive coach?

Typically brought in by HR departments, senior managers, and even the coaching clients themselves, executive coaching is reserved for those who are critical to an organization's success (CEOs, CTOs, CFOs and other top-tier leaders).But recently we are also seeing executive coaching being employed to support new and aspiring leaders as well. Its value is reflected in a range of recent press ranging from *Forbes* to the *Harvard Business Review* (HBR).

In an article titled "What can coaches do for you?" the *Harvard Business Review* found that forty-eight percent of executive coaches are reportedly hired to "develop high potentials or facilitate transition," followed by twenty-six percent who are engaged to "act as a sounding board."[2] "Addressing derailing behavior" registered a distant third, with only twelve percent of executive coaches hired for this purpose.

These findings represent a shift in the industry, as well as those seeking coaching. Many executives who now get the most out of your services are those who possess a "fierce desire to learn and grow," according to the HBR article. (Uh… hello, dream client! Who wouldn't want to work with someone like that!?)

Within this role, you work alongside directors, vice presidents, managing directors, or other senior leaders of a company or nonprofit organization. You often focus on developing leadership skills and capacity, with highly positive, purpose-driven business results typically being the end goal.

---

2 Coutu, Diane, and Carol Kauffman. 2009. "What Can Coaches Do for You." *Harvard Business Review* 87 (1): 91-97.

Should you specialize as an executive coach?

This branch of coaching isn't for everyone. But if you possess strong business and leadership experience and have a passion for the inner workings of high-level corporate life, the answer is a resounding YES! You could get the chance to work side by side with some of the world's most influential business leaders, helping them shape the companies that in turn shape our world.

In pursuing this branch of coaching, you identify as someone who loves to serve high-profile leaders and decision makers — recently in particular those who are up-and-coming. Like small business coaches, executive coaches often possess additional experience or expertise in a given industry or role within a company that they use in combination with coaching. With this background knowledge and history, you are far more effective at assisting leaders by addressing the needs of that company. Additionally, many people come to us with degrees in leadership development and organization development, wanting to add coaching into their toolkit to shine up their skills and move their résumé to the top of the stack.

In fact, many an executive coach started out in organization development, HR, training and development, or is a former CEO or comparable leader themselves. Above all, they have notable experience in the corporate arena. They can demonstrate a clear methodology for developing others and readily create a unique model that specifically addresses the individual executive and the challenges they face. If that's you, executive coaching is one of the most effective ways to transition into a consulting-type position or simply boost your profile within your current organization.

An important subcategory that deserves mention here is the executive coach with a focus on nonprofits. Like a standard executive coach, it's helpful to have background and work experience in the nonprofit arena. But it's also not uncommon for business professionals to branch out into helping these kinds of organizations. At Coach Training World, we routinely have a broad range of individuals interested in the nonprofit world, or who are already well established within it, seek coach training. So if you're on the hunt for a tribe that's passionate about community foundations, company-sponsored foundations and corporate giving programs, cooperative ventures, endowments or private foundations, it's a fair bet you'll find more than a few kindred, charity-minded spirits here.

Meet Yvonne Chang

Starting over is never easy. It's especially hard when you're recovering physically from an accident, and even more so when transitioning from one culture to another. Yvonne has experience with both.

On a sunny day in southern California, she was biking with her beau before heading back to college when her life changed in an instant. Caught alongside a large semi-truck, the front wheel of her bike wavered and got caught in the double tires of the truck. Yvonne woke to emergency paramedics, a team of doctors, and eight weeks at Huntington Beach Hospital for rehabilitation. This was followed by many more months of upheaval as she worked through the physical and emotional pain.

It was a long road to get back into the world. Yet along the way, she discovered a few insights. Yvonne uncovered a radiant, internal power that now serves as her constant driving force when anything gets tough. She also came to realize how precious life is and that it should never be wasted. When she mixed her internal power, creativity and sense of self-responsibility and applied it towards a deeper purpose, her life gained real meaning.

Yvonne is a true Renaissance woman. She possesses a broad range of experience in other pursuits that include fashion design and apparel product management, dance and performing arts, modeling, beauty, the natural world, and ecopsychology.

She started her journey toward becoming a professional coach as an "ontwikkelings begeleider," an executive leadership guide in The Netherlands. For twenty-three years, she was co-owner of Kinhem Organization Advisors Network. Within this role, she developed her coaching practice for corporate, government and business leaders, as well as professionals and individuals of different ages and occupations. While working with people from Indonesia, she focused special attention on their culture-based struggles to adapt to life in Holland.

As a certified Whole Person Coach, Yvonne uses the tools and techniques of coaching to reinforce and deepen the impact of her services. Her advanced certification adds a level of credibility that ensures she is alignment with the industry's best practices and standards. It also gives her peace of mind. Yvonne is highly cognizant of the fact that she is working with people's lives, careers and businesses. Therefore, holistic alignment is critical.

These highly developed skills enable her to help professionals discover their capacity to step into leadership for more impact, success and mastery over their career frontier. At the same time, her capacity as a Whole Person Coach enables her to help her clients integrate their own professional, personal and cultural identities.

> "[Whole Person Coaching] has enabled me to help individuals find in themselves the kind of value, meaning and grounding that it took me years to find in myself," Yvonne says. "Through coaching, I can consolidate my experiences and studies into a personalized plan and approach matched to each client's needs and aspirations."

Today, Yvonne continues to expand her business, offering services locally and regionally, while continuing on an exclusive-need basis with her clients in the Netherlands. As the successful solopreneur of Yvonne Chang Consulting, she connects with people who are at a turning point, have hit a plateau, or get a wake-up call. Rather than narrowing the dialogue with clients to one specific choice or decision, she helps them step back, find a higher perch, and see themselves from the perspective of the universe.

Through one-on-one sessions, workshops and group programs, Yvonne assists her professional clients plan with expanded vision and a firmer sense of purpose, creating what she has termed "Radiant Power Leaders."

> "Perhaps because most of my clients are women, I've discovered that the term "radiant power leadership" (RPL) seems to strike a chord," she says. "Radiance is about bringing your inner light out into the world. It suggests a confident energy that draws people in as it shines outward with warmth and vibrancy. Furthermore, RPL is about the power to engage and elevate others as opposed to a more traditional view of holding power over others."

In addition to coaching sessions, you can find Yvonne creating a range of empowering trainings/workshops, presentations and courses. She also initiates and organizes leadership-empowerment events and conferences for women, and in particular women of color.

Team Coaching

As a team coach, you provide the tools and dialog that enable people to work together more productively and effectively toward an agreed-upon performance objective. In this role, you champion communication, team development, conflict resolution and better self-understanding to improve workplace relationships. And though it's not always the case, some leadership development and executive coaches also offer team coaching in addition to their standard services.

Your mission is to not only streamline the work process but also make it more enjoyable for all involved. Highly valuable in today's business environment, this process has been shown to noticeably boost individual and team output toward greater company success and optimal work environments.

At its core, team coaching is about interpersonal skills and improved interactions within a group, recognizing that performance issues may still exist despite the presence of high-performing individuals. While you may employ breakout sessions in which a single individual receives focused attention, this branch of coaching is more concerned with the entire work group or organization.

Who works with a team coach?

Team coaches are hired when a team or group leader seeks to increase their effectiveness and productivity. From corporations, governmental agencies and nonprofit organizations to private communities, these teams seek a custom-tailored approach that addresses their specific needs to reach the most successful outcome. Here are a few of the challenges and opportunities you could be hired for:

- Establishing expectations for behavior
- Team performance
- Effective communication
- Creating or revising systems for individual reward and recognition
- Offering support and insight, allowing the team to reach strategic objectives in direct alignment with organizational values
- Organizational growth and development
- Conflict management
- Process improvement

Should you specialize as a team coach?

Those who are drawn to this branch of the coaching profession have a knack for clarifying a wide range of contrary viewpoints and creating a system that meets the team's desired vision for effective collaboration. Like any other coaching modality, you must be able to step aside and allow your client(s) to lead by taking responsibility for their own development.

Coaches who operate successfully in this field often have experience with group coaching or working with groups of people in a workplace environment. But that's not a hard and fast rule. You may also have executive coaching experience or academic training related to team development. Others that prosper in team coaching have pursued academic interests in communication, group dynamics, and conflict management, to name just a few of the most common disciplines.

Most importantly, you should enjoy working with diverse groups of people and tackling the complex nature of corporate culture and business systems.

Meet Justin Cassens

Justin emerged from college ready to take on the world. But like so many young people today, he couldn't find work that aligned with his skills and earnest desire to help others. He struggled to find a job that took advantage of his degree in communication, fit into the schedule he wanted for life, and wasn't an unbearable daily grind. Finding this combination became a considerable challenge within most corporate settings. He spent months looking and interviewing, only to be discouraged by the limitations of what the job market could provide. That's when Justin discovered coaching.

> *"I was pointed toward life coaching when I told someone my ideal job would be working as a professional friend,"* he says.

He'd never considered becoming his own boss. But after receiving encouragement from his father (a business owner himself), Justin began exploring the entrepreneurial path. Coaching has turned out to be his dream-come-true career. It satisfies all his work-life balance requirements and enables him to do something he genuinely loves.

Like many others who are drawn to the coaching profession, Justin has been "coaching" others for most of his life. Rich in perspective, he was the guy all the girls called their "best friend" in high school and college. But it wasn't until he received Whole Person coach training that he discovered he could do more than just be a sympathetic ear for friends.

Justin has quickly established himself as a secret weapon for college graduates in their late twenties to early thirties who want to feel more comfortable, confident and at choice in their social lives – especially women who feel they don't have a voice in important matters.

> *"I help find a direction where there was none. I help find the words needed for expression. I help find the possibilities that were hidden. Whether it's finding a way to be able to say "no" to friends, finding comfort with loved ones, or finding new ways to stand out at work." (Courtesy of coachtrainingworld.com)* [3]

For years, Justin has been the best-kept-secret for those who find themselves in the background and want to be seen, heard and respected for who they are. Now he uses the tools and methodology of Whole Person coaching to find real solutions to problems, creating a sustainable approach his clients can use to reinforce confidence on their own.

Today Justin works primarily with those who want to improve their understanding of communication and

---

3 Coach Training World. n.d. "Introducing Justin Cassens, Life Coach." Accessed April 4, 2018. https://coachtrainingworld.com/justin-cassens-life-coach-salem-oregon.

acquire skills to master social settings. He supports people in finding ways to counter negative thoughts, fearlessly self-express, and realize how capable they truly are. Through in-person and web-based sessions, Justin helps his clients discover how to get the most out of their relationships – including friendships, romantic involvements, and professional contacts – enabling them to enjoy life to the fullest.

> *"Freely sharing appreciation with the people around us will help make the world a better place, and I can't get enough of people who share that point of view," Justin says. "I can't imagine anything better than working to help people realize their full potential."*

Spiritual Coaching

Spiritual coaching can take many forms. By training to become a Whole Person Coach, you'll ultimately shape the foundation of your coaching practice upon your spiritual or religious preferences. This is how you will attract your ideal clients.

As a spiritual coach, your clients gain access to the inner guidance that lives within. Drawing upon their unique way of connecting with the divine, their belief system is the starting point for your work. Through their beliefs, you then offer them a myriad of tools, techniques and spiritual practices.

By connecting with the divine wisdom of an individual's spirit, you help your clients identify and remove any barriers standing in the way of their path to happiness, fulfillment and life success.

Who works with a spiritual coach?

Many believe in the presence of a higher power. This is described by many names, including God, The Divine, Source or Collective Conscious, to name a few. Regardless of how your clients refer to their particular system of belief, they desire a deeper understanding of themselves, their purpose and true potential. As a spiritual coach, your clients seek to work with you side-by-side as they access their spiritual insight and connection. You accompany them as they course-correct their life direction onto the path that is most meaningful to them and in direct alignment with their inner guidance and resources.

A popular subcategory of spiritual coaching is divine manifestation. Those who identify with *The Secret* by Rhonda Byrne, *Law of Attraction* by Michael Losier and similar titles centered on personal transformation often desire to work with a spiritual coach. Like the pathways found in these bestsellers, clients are most interested in tapping into the energy and vibrations that lead to manifestation.

Should you specialize as a spiritual coach?

The drive to seek meaning and our purpose in life is part of what it means to be human. Operating within this framework, many individuals who specialize in spiritual coaching tend to have a spiritual background themselves. Among many others, this may include a background in ministry or a similar form of spiritual training or practice such as Buddhism, Hinduism (Yogis), or meditation. In the same way, other successful spiritual coaches have employed tarot, astrology, intuitive readings and complementary tools to help their clients find their own way.

Also, interesting to note is a growing interest in spiritual coaching by practitioners of specific religious creeds. For one reason or another, they no longer wish to continue with the particular dogma or ritualized practices of the religion. But they have not let go of their faith. Training to become a spiritual coach allows them to keep in touch with this aspect of self while helping others do the same.

Though it is not necessary for you to share the same system of beliefs with your clients, shared beliefs may lead to greater levels of success in some cases. Nevertheless, as someone who understands the deeper dimensions and multiple access points to the divine, you are well-equipped to support your clients in a myriad of ways. The cornerstone to your success within this niche is an understanding and acceptance of the belief systems of your clients, as well as your commitment to help them access the divine as they define it.

Like all other branches of coaching, spiritual coaches are soul-driven individuals who delight in helping clients attain their best possible future on a soul level. Unlike other coaching niches however, this branch places the soul's yearning and spiritual fulfillment front and center. It taps into an individual's divine connection and gifts as the primary source of wisdom.

Further subsets of this niche are found in those who enhance their spiritual coaching services with a focus on:

- Energy and vibrational fields
- Imagery and soul collage
- Intuitive painting

- Manifestation
- Divination
- Soul work
- Shamanism and spiritual journeys
- And an extensive range of specialized rituals and practices that serve individual belief systems

Meet Jonathan Crews

Inspired by his early exposure to the Vedic wisdom of India, Jonathan has dedicated his life to pursing personal and collective transformation. He has spent more than forty-five years offering people the techniques and processes that raise consciousness and provide an effective system for life-guidance.

Like many successful individuals who use coaching to complement and enhance their services, Jonathan was looking for a context to support his astrology clients on a more ongoing basis. The problem is that many astrology clients only tend to seek out readings on a semi-annual to annual basis. But when considering the knowledge and wisdom Jonathan has accumulated over the course of his life, he knew he could do more to guide people toward the evolution of their soul and their purpose in this incarnation. That's where coaching came in.

"Professional coaching has been a wonderful adjunct to what I currently do," he says. "It assists people in discovering their purpose and unfolding the gifts they are meant to give in this life. Practical yet profound, it's a vehicle for helping people bring into manifestation their heart's desires. But manifesting those goals is

generally not something that gets accomplished in one session. It takes time and a committed support system to help a client bring them to fruition."

Jonathan's mission is to assist those who are interested in greater self-understanding. Unafraid to confront the challenges they face in life, most of his clients are dedicated to making the world a better place as they fulfill their life's purpose.

With degrees in psychology and a master's in business administration, Jonathan also has training in body-centered psychotherapuetic techniques. In addition, he has spent the last fifteen years practicing Vedic astrology, the oldest and most preeminent form of life guidance. Commonly known as Jyotish (which translates as "Lords of Light", referring to the planets and stars), he uses this ancient predictive science to accurately identify a person's strengths, gifts and talents, as well as their challenges in life.

By combining an initial Vedic astrological life guidance reading with the concepts of professional coaching, he can work with individuals on a more intimate and extended basis. This approach helps his clients focus their awareness on the practical steps that can be taken to manifest the gifts and talents identified in their Vedic chart.

Yet despite his professional accreditations and advanced learning, Jonathan also frequently credits a teacher much closer to home: his wife, Brii. Attending Whole Person coach training as a couple, Jonathan and Brii (a practicing psychotherapist) were looking for a way to take their individual practices to a higher level of effectiveness. And though they each apply the tools and techniques of coaching in a unique way, their joint training has enabled them to deepen the learning for one another.

> *"My wife, Brii, has been one of my greatest teachers. We have learned the importance of communication and conflict resolution. This perspective allows us to consciously manage our differences while celebrating the dreams and aspirations we hold so dear. Most importantly, we honor the reflection the other gives both positive and challenging as a gift from Spirit that enables us to walk the path of Love." (Courtesy of jonathancrews.com)*

Today Jonathan specializes in solving problems related to emotional expression, relationships, career and finances, health and well-being, and egoic identification – all of which have the potential to create suffering in our lives when out of alignment with our true purpose.

> *"Over time, I recognized a tendency among spiritual seekers to "transcend" the more painful aspects of our emotional lives. This contributes to a marked lack of integration. Rather than turn away from our wounds, I found it far more beneficial to compassionately accept and embrace them as the foundation for transformation." (Courtesy of jonathancrews.com)[4]*

In addition to his consultations, he also routinely lectures on the benefits of meditation and, as a certified instructor, teaches courses in meditation and yoga on a regular basis. For those interested in learning more about Vedic astrology, Jonathan gives presentations on Vedic philosophy and the nature and purpose of the practice as put forth by the ancient seers of India.

---

4 Crews, Jonathan. n.d. "About Jonathan Crews." *About Jonathan Crews.* Accessed April 4, 2018. https://jonathancrews.wordpress.com/about.

Relationship Coaching

Relationship coaching runs a wide gamut. On any given day, you may have sessions with singles and married couples as well as divorcées. Regardless of the client, you strive to help people discover their best self and the right actions to create the love, connection and ease inside their most important relationships.

Depending on your specific focus, you support your clients to be true to themselves, identify their needs and desires, and express their feelings with others. You may also introduce your clients to resources that enable them to better negotiate the complexity and dynamic nature of interpersonal relationships.

Most relationship coaches focus on intimate relationships. However, some opt to help people with personal challenges such as personal power, boundaries, self-esteem, social anxiety, effective communication, and similar difficulties encountered when dealing with others in daily life.

Who works with a relationship coach?

Expect a variety of people to seek out your services as a relationship coach. But keep in mind, the most successful coaches within this niche are specific about the challenges they help others with.

For example, if you become a dating coach, clients seek your support and guidance on the best ways to find the right mate. If you choose to work with divorcees, your clients may want to explore ways to recreate their life after a divorce. Those who want to help widowers may offer ways to connect with someone new after years of being "off the market." And if you are interested in helping couples deepen and improve their relationship, you may offer strategies and communication tools that help them with intimacy issues and express their needs more openly.

Regardless of the branch you choose, expect those who knock on your door to have had some form of self-realization. In all likelihood, they recognize their connection with someone specific or others in general is at risk. If you work with couples, the risk is likely to the relationship. If you work with individuals like divorcees or widowers, the risk is more centered on the individuals themselves, their potential for long-term happiness, and a fear that it may escape them if they continue down their current path.

Should you specialize as a relationship coach?

If you love helping others become their best self within a relationship, this coaching pathway might be for you. Relationship coaches tend to immerse themselves in books like *Attached* by Amir Levine and Rachel Heller or *The 5 Love Languages* series by Gary Chapman. They readily see potential for connection and depth of human experience within relationships, recognizing the importance for couples and individuals to be able to more effectively relate and communicate with one another.

As a relationship coach, you bring your own relationship experience and wisdom into the mix as you help others. Maybe you've learned that the most important relationship you've got is the one you hold with yourself. Now you want to help others remain true and authentic in their interactions with others. Perhaps you've been through a complex relationship and discovered successful ways to resolve differences or simply extricate yourself and move on. Regardless of the subset you choose to pursue, the knowledge you possess has tremendous value. This is true whether you've obtained it through personal experience, professional training, or some other form of counseling you currently provide.

Relationship coaches are heart- and soul-centered individuals who delight in helping their clients attain the deepest, most meaningful connections with themselves and others. These core relationships serve as a conduit for connecting to one's whole self.

Although this niche is referred to as relationship coaching, it is similar to life coaching in that you may touch upon everything in the life of an individual or couple. This spectrum often ranges from health and long-term happiness to money matters and even the division of labor within a relationship.

Further subsets within this niche are seen in those who enhance their relationship coaching services with a focus on:

- Non-Violent Communication
- Divorce/Heartbreak Coaching
- Dating Coaching
- Marital Coaching
- Pre-Marital Coaching
- Love Languages
- Emotional Intelligence
- Intimacy Skills
- Authentic Communication

Meet Michelle Anita Wirta

Michelle has had many upheavals in her personal and professional life. They shook much of the foundation she thought defined her. As she'll tell you: the nagging disquiet of uncertainty acted as one of the primary guardians to her early success.

With a strong background in clinical psychology and women's studies, Michelle also specializes in holistic healing modalities, dance fitness and the arts. Unfortunately, when she was well into her graduate program, she discovered clinical psychology wasn't where her heart was at. Suddenly faced with the prospect of a career that did not engage her, she began searching for a framework that allowed space for positive psychology in combination with active, intentional transformation. That's when she discovered coaching.

> *"Becoming a Whole Person Coach helped me bring my core passions together in a way that benefits people greatly," Michelle says. "In turn, it also allows me to run a business that is my true calling."*

Since becoming a coach in 2006, Michelle has crafted a successful online coaching business as The Soul Translator. She combines purpose and identity coaching with a profound process for deep spiritual validation and energetic clearing. She primarily works with women who identify themselves in one of two ways:

- Highly Driven – Women craving to reconnect with the feminine, spiritual, and intuitive side in their personal lives then translate that into how they run their companies or new entrepreneurial endeavors.

- Highly Sensitive People (HSPs) – Women who want to learn how to be powerful and prosperous by being themselves and doing things their way instead of becoming someone else they think they need to be to earn acceptance, success, and happiness.

Michelle also uses coaching to help her clients integrate and activate the self-awareness and growth they experience through Soul Translations. This unique branch of coaching uses tarot as a representative and intuitive system to help individuals and business owners create sustainable change and broaden their self-awareness.

These offerings are representative of Michelle's most impressive achievements: she has embraced who she truly is and successfully brought all of herself into play!

After graduating from Coach Training World, she began to grow her services as a life coach by specializing in limiting beliefs and self-esteem. She then added other modalities that reflected her love of energetics and healing, later branching into identity and branding.

Today, Michelle is tapping her highly intuitive capacities as she creates a Sheroes Journey Tarot Deck, a wordplay book for kids and adults, and a book about soul translation.

> *"Coaching's tools and processes enable me to seamlessly bring my clients to identify with who they really are,"* she says. *"We then extend that insight into a business that can match, express, and serve them as an extension of their genuine desires."*

Which direction is right for you?

The niches discussed in detail within this chapter are just a few of the countless variations and combinations available to you. Where there's a need, there's a niche. That's the beauty of professional coaching: it allows you as the coach to take what you are most passionate about and share your wisdom with others. As a result, the opportunities for a specialty coaching practice are as diverse as those who practice them.

Examples include:

- Academic Coaching
- Adoption Coaching
- ADD/ADHD Coaching
- Addictions and Recovery Coaching
- Alternative Schooling Coaching
- Attachment Parenting Coaching
- Animal Coaching
- Anti-aging Coaching
- Artist and Creative Coaching
- Asthma and Allergies Coaching
- Attorney Coaching
- Autism Spectrum Coaching
- Alternative Health Coaching
- Anxiety Coaching
- Asian-American Coaching
- Athletic Coaching
- Birthing/Doula Coaching

- Business Coaching
- Cancer Coaching
- Career Coaching
- Christian Coaching
- Communications Coaching
- Conflict Coaching
- Cooking Coaching
- Co-Parenting Coaching
- Confidence Coaching
- Couples Coaching
- Cultural Relationships Coaching
- Diabetes Coaching
- Digital Marketing Coaching
- Divine Calling Coaching
- Divorce Coaching
- Educator Coaching
- Emotional Freedom Techniques (EFT) Coaching
- Emotional Intelligence Coaching
- Empowerment Coaching
- End-of-Life Coaching
- Engineering Coaching
- Entrepreneur Coaching
- Essential Oils Coaching
- Ethics Coaching
- Etiquette Coaching

- Executive Coaching
- Financial Coaching
- Gen-X Coaching
- Gluten-Free Diet Coaching
- Grief Coaching
- Financial Coaching
- Herbal Coaching
- Hair, Make-up and Clothing Coaching
- Holistic Life Coaching
- Home Environment Coaching
- Hypnotherapy Coaching
- Interior Design Coaching
- Intimacy/Sex Coaching
- Introvert/HSP Coaching
- Job Interview Coaching
- Law of Attraction Coaching
- Leadership Coaching
- LGBTQ Coaching
- Life Coaching
- Life Purpose Coaching
- Life Skills Coaching
- Living Abroad Coaching
- Make-up Coaching
- Manufacturing Coaching
- Marketing Coaching
- Meditation Coaching

- Mid-life Change Coaching
- Military Coaching
- Millennial Coaching
- Money Coaching
- Motivational Coaching
- Nature Coaching
- Native American Coaching
- NLP Coaching
- Non-Violent Coaching
- Nutrition Coaching
- Communication Coaching
- Nursing Coaching
- Online Business Coaching
- Organizing Coaching
- Organizational Coaching
- Parenting Coaching
- Performance/Effectiveness Coaching
- Performing Arts Coaching
- Personal Development Coaching
- Physician Coaching
- Political Coaching
- Procrastination Coaching
- Product Development Coaching
- Raw/Vegan or Vegetarian Coaching
- Reiki Coaching
- Rebirthing Coaching

- Relationship Coaching
- Resiliency Coaching
- Sales Coaching
- Self-Esteem Coaching
- Singles Coaching
- Social Media Coaching
- Soul Coaching
- Speaking Coaching
- Special Needs Coaching
- Spiritual Coaching
- Spiritual Entrepreneur Coaching
- Start-up Coaching
- Stress Management Coaching
- Success Coaching
- Succession Planning Coaching
- Team-building Coaching
- Technology Coaching
- Teenage/Young Adult Coaching
- Time Management Coaching
- Transformational Coaching
- Transitions Coaching
- Travel Coaching
- Veterinary Coaching
- Volunteer Coordinator Coaching
- Wedding Planner Coaching
- Weight-loss Coaching

- Wellness Coaching
- Whole Person Coaching
- Whole Life Coaching
- Work/Life Balance Coaching
- Yoga Coaching

Create a niche that is uniquely you

Perhaps you don't see yourself fitting into one of these categories. Not to worry – that's not uncommon. The good news is that, as a Whole Person Coach, you can choose who you serve and what you call yourself. It's another one of the amazing perks of this universal modality. Want to become a doula coach? Equine coach? Or vegan coach? Whatever lights your fire can become your specialty. It's entirely up to you!

The reason Whole Person Coaching fits so well into so many different applications is that it's a meta-process. It amplifies your existing gifts, talents, experience and expertise making it possible for you to evoke sustainable and transformational change in others. For this reason, you'll find it as the shaping force behind individual lives and businesses across the globe.

Choosing the type of coaching you offer can feel like a big decision. But it's also an opportunity for you create your own parameters. You pave the way. So I challenge you to explore what your own dream-come-true career or business would look and feel like, connecting your passions and expertise to your ideal audience.

Chapter review and coming attractions

In this chapter, we looked at some of the most popular types of coaching. We also saw examples of real-life change makers who are passionately making their difference in the world. The true inspiration from these success stories is just how adaptable Whole Person Coaching can be. Remember: where there's a need, there's a niche. As a Whole Person Coach, you decide what you are most passionate about then share that wisdom with others. There are no limits on your ability to create a specialty coaching practice that is truly reflective of who you are and caters directly to those you want to help.

Next Up: Now that you're familiar with the numerous options you have as a professional coach, it's time to discover how you can maximize your time and financial potential through the Spiral Growth Coaching Business Model. More importantly, you'll learn the three main ways you can profit from your passions while changing lives (starting with your own!).

~ In Your Journal ~

We've covered a lot of territory in this chapter. But don't get overwhelmed. We're here to move you forward at your own pace, one step at a time. Also bear in mind that, as you train to become a coach, you'll get radically clear on your niche – that's one of the best parts of coach training.

For now, start playing with the possibilities available to you. As you can see, Whole Person Coaching makes it possible for you to coach a wide variety of people on an endless array of topics. This enables you to become a coach without the worry of perfecting your niche right away. It also affords the luxury of changing directions in your coaching business later if desired – even if that only means adding services or veering slightly into one area more than another. With this in mind…

- Without too much pressure to make a final decision, reflect on the various types of coaching we've discussed. Now write down two to three areas that feel most exciting to you.

- Next, decide how you might like to further specialize in each category. Let your pen flow and see what you come up with. Talk with friends and family. Ask what kind of coaching they think you might be best at.

~6~

Be Exponential: From impact to income

Exponential. It's a word you hear often in coaching circles. Many times, it's in reference to your clients and their individual growth (thanks to you!). But it also represents your potential as a business owner.

Coaching enables you to impact countless lives simply by contributing your best to the world. It is also the only career path that recognizes your unlimited potential, rewarding you with versatility and scalability you can't get in any other profession.

My first entrepreneurial venture as a professional coach was as The Good Living Guide. Working with a diverse client base, I incorporated life coaching with personal training to form a unique offering at the time. This enabled me to provide a rich suite of services that immediately amplified my client's results and my earnings.

With the rapid growth of my business, my free time began to dwindle – ironic really, since work-life balance was one of the most shared challenges my clients had! Before long, my workhorse identity buried me deep into the trenches of my business. My days were fueled by non-fat lattes as I tried to manage my overwhelming client base and schedule. Without even realizing it, I had traded away much of my precious time and had left nothing with which to live in other areas of my life.

Work-life balance issues aside, it was deeply rewarding to operate individually with clients in the early stages of my coaching business. It enabled me to master my coaching capacity as my expertise grew. After having what felt like the same conversations day after day, I recognized common themes inherent in the challenges my clients faced. Seeing these patterns, I chose to leverage my most effective coaching strategies to create a group coaching program. Not only did I give myself an immediate pay raise that day, but my clients prospered from the supportive nature of the group environment and community that formed within.

Build a career and business that grows with you

My first coaching venture taught me a valuable lesson: the importance of a business model that maximizes time while increasing the number of people served. The obvious benefit though was far more than financial.

The capacity to serve hundreds of clients simultaneously was absolutely amazing. But it was by happenstance that I gravitated from coaching individuals to groups, then eventually into creating my own coaching products. Had I known back then what I know now, I would have planned the future of my coaching business in advance.

Spiral Growth Coaching Business Model

At Coach Training World, we use the Spiral Growth Business Model as a way to encourage our students to plan, build and grow their coaching businesses. Using this model, you can fulfill your dream of working side by side with clients with the option to supplement your income through group coaching, online products and services. This will enable you to maximize your time and your financial potential, both essential elements to becoming a successful coach.

Much like it sounds, this model is what clearly defines what you'll offer your clients in terms of coaching services. The idea is that for every service you offer, you'll have a complementary upgrade, thereby generating a long-term, high-value relationship.

For example, your individual clients could join you on a retreat. Or they could purchase your digital programs as a companion to the learning they'll experience working with you in person. Similarly, your online group program could be leveraged to increase your individual client base by addressing individual needs that don't necessarily fit within the group dynamic.

In essence, you are spiraling up the level and depth of service you offer while increasing your financial sustainability.

To design your own ideal business model, you'll want to first decide how you'd like to deliver your coaching services. From here, you'll quickly see how you can grow your business to generate the impact and income you desire.

No matter where your unique brilliance lies, there are three main ways you can profit from your passions while changing lives:

1. One-on-one coaching
2. Group coaching
3. Coaching programs or products

One-on-one coaching

Newer coaches are often drawn to the comfort of working privately with their clients. Simplicity and expediency are two of the main reasons. Although trust, intimacy and rapport are equally necessary in a group setting, they're often easiest to cultivate within a one-on-one partnership. Privacy and confidential space lessen the vulnerability that can arise in a group environment. This is true of clients and coaches alike.

With the advancements in technology, individual coaching can happen from just about anywhere there is a cellular or Internet connection. Coaching sessions are frequently conducted over the phone or online through Skype, FaceTime and Zoom to name a few. These delivery options allow you to work from just about anywhere in the world, including your own home.

The upside to working individually with your clients is the depth and speed that often result from the personal nature and singular attention of this format. Working one-on-one enables you to quickly recognize your client's needs and shift your approach accordingly.

If you are introverted or sensitive to group energy, identify as highly sensitive or an empath, you'll appreciate the ease and comfort of working one-on-one with your ideal clients. Even though group coaching is currently popular and profitable, individual coaching can be just as lucrative should you market yourself well.

Here are a few tips on how you can set yourself up for success coaching individuals:

Client workload

Transition into your coaching business by setting aside one or two days a week for clients. As your client base expands, add additional time as desired. If you are newer to coaching, those numbers might feel light. But as your own boss, you'll be wearing additional hats beyond "coach." You'll want to ensure you have ample time to grow your business as well as work in it. This is especially true if you are in start-up mode.

Where many coaches see an average of eight to fifteen individual clients per week, it's up to you on how you want to fill your coaching days. The amount you charge per session will also play a big factor in the number of clients you'll see. Quality over quantity has always been one of my best practices.

Client commitment

Research shows a typical coaching relationship lasts from three to five months, typically meeting three to four times a month.

Enrolling your prospective clients into a longer-term relationship lends to the success rate of the coaching process. Trust builds with time, and so does the momentum of the coaching process. The results your clients achieve will be more sustainable, and the financial stability of your coaching enterprise will be enhanced.

Seasoned coaches often retain their clients for years on an as-needed basis. I personally enjoy having clients who come back to work with me as their life or needs shift. I've worked with some individuals on and off for as long as thirteen years. This is not only good for your business, it's also amazing to witness someone's life unfolding and the treasures they discover along the way.

Session length

The length and frequency of the sessions you offer are essentially up to you and, at times, your clients. This is especially true if you coach inside larger companies. The average coaching session length ranges from twenty to ninety minutes.

This is one of the many customizable features of the delivery method. The only "right way" is the one that works for you and your clients. Consider offering sessions that provide you with the flexibility and freedom you want in your schedule while effectively meeting your clients' needs.

Key questions to consider when deciding session length:

- **How much time is my "ideal client" willing to invest in a session?** Keep in mind that a busy corporate leader may opt for a thirty-minute session, whereas someone working through identifying their next career step might want to devote ninety minutes a week to figuring out their ideal situation.

- **How much time is ideal to facilitate a complete coaching session?** The best way to answer this is to start coaching and take note of the time in relation to results. If you're allocating too much, you'll find yourself casting around for topics to fill time toward the end. Too little and you or your client will feel rushed and dissatisfied with the results. One of the easiest ways to gauge the time limit of an ideal session is to ask your clients if they feel they had enough time. Then adjust accordingly.

- **How often do you plan to meet with your clients?** If you are meeting them every week versus once a month, that might inform the length of your sessions.

Financial investment

Don't shortchange yourself here: your experience has real value! You are selling a transformation, not your time. Repeat: You are NOT selling your time! Depending on your level of individual experience and specialization, you can charge fees ranging between $75 and $500+ per session. That said, I've met and personally worked with clients willing to invest top dollar – $20,000 to $100,000 – in the right coach for exclusivity and expertise.

These numbers are affected by factors that include: who you serve, their income and geographic location. Your marketing and perceived worth also play a gigantic role in what you receive for your services. In fact, marketing is a key component to your success as a coach, especially when it comes to getting paid what you are worth.

Private coaching can easily consume a lot of your time. For this reason, I recommend you establish fees that enable you to sustain your good work in the world.

Prospering in the world of one-on-one coaching

The beauty of being your own boss is you can create the rules on how things are done and change them as you go. You don't have to follow or recreate someone else's way of working – this is your business now!

Employ effective time management techniques

While there are numerous ways to save time and money, a few of the most basic things that have helped me over the years are:

- Coach on the phone or online versus heading to an office – no travel time required
- Consolidate your schedule to serve clients two to three days a week (being sure to leave enough self-care space in between appointments)
- Invite your clients to choose a preferred day and time, and schedule recurring appointments a month in advance

Again, the possibilities are endless. By scheduling yourself well in advance you not only free up your time to continue building your business, you take back the free time that's often missing in so many of our lives. Want to go for a hike, take a road trip, or write a novel? Scheduling in advance and using convenient channels of communication are what can help you get there.

Give yourself a raise – same audience, different location

If you live in or near a major metropolitan area, chances are your clients are easily within walking or driving distance. But not everyone lives near a major city.

Does that mean you should give up on your dream of becoming a coach? Of course not. Maybe you live in a small town that is economically challenged. In this setting, many people may not immediately recognize the value of coaching or are averse to spending money on what they view as an intangible service. Branch out.

One solution could be relocation. But for most of us, that's not a viable or even a desirable option. Why not coach online or over the phone instead? Create a marketing plan that targets major markets and leverage the internet to find your ideal clients. Take Richard for example.

After struggling for years with the limited financial resources of those in his local area, Richard shifted his client base from the Midwest to Los Angeles. Honing in on his specific audience through online marketing, Richard tapped into a different geographic location, and positioned himself as the go-to coach who had a track record of proven results (underpaid though he had been up to that point).

There are always workarounds to getting paid what you are worth. A slight change in "where" or "how" you find your clients may be all you need. Ironically, when he told me about his strategy, I was a bit skeptical. But then I got introduced to the LA and NY markets. He's right!

Create a coaching package

Another popular way of bolstering your income through individual coaching is to create a coaching package. Coaching packages offer slightly reduced rates for bundled sessions that come in three-, five- or ten-session packages. The reduction in per-session rate is a way to encourage clients to commit to their long-term progress.

But don't stop there. Give your coaching package a results-based name. It should imply the outcome your clients could achieve should they choose to work with you.

For example, you might have the "Blissfully Married" coaching package, or offer a workshop like "Live Your Genius." A couple more examples could be "Profit from Your Passions" or "Embody Health." These titles convey the end result, the takeaway, thus making tangible what to some people may seem intangible at first glance.

Remember (and never forget to remind your prospective clients): change is rarely an overnight success. You can use coaching packages as a means of long-term support. This enables your clients to confidently reach their goals and produce the results they desire, knowing they can rely on you until they get there. It also allows you to relax a bit, secure in the knowledge you have income coming in for months at a time.

Start your own coaching firm

I might be putting the cart before the horse, but many coaches are also visionaries! If you are a true believer in the power of working one-on-one but don't want to be limited by your time, start your own coaching firm. Christa King is one such example.

Christa discovered, after working with individual clients for a couple years, that she possessed natural visionary tendencies. She was more at home as the CEO in her own company using her coaching skills to develop others inside her company. Today Christa partners with other changemakers to offer coaching and other related services to a larger client base in her company, Fitlandia. She employs her coaching skills both as a company leader and a group leader for her select clients.

Other considerations for one-on-one sessions

If you aren't coaching on the phone or online, and don't want to work in coffee shops due to privacy concerns, you'll need an office to conduct your sessions in. A home office can often fit the bill quite nicely. Alternatively, you can rent or share space with other people, splitting the cost.

Another option is to work on site with your clients. But you'll want to take into consideration commute time and availability of private, uninterrupted space.

Individual and group coaching hybrid business models

One of the more innovative coaching models I've encountered was conducted by one of my writing mentors. Tea offers a yearlong program for thirty-six people. Each month, this group breaks up into four to six smaller groups that shift members every month. In addition to her groups, she provides twelve thirty-minute private coaching sessions for all her participants. Not only does this enable Tea to offer a one-year program, guaranteeing a reliable source of revenue twelve months in advance, it also provides her community constant contact with new and brilliant minds over a longer period of time. You can see the added benefit of working with her one-on-one throughout the year.

As a result of her innovative model, Tea's clients are far more successful. Her services are further amplified by the motivation created through group interactions. With this in mind, let's explore how you can add group coaching into your suite of services.

Group coaching

Adding group coaching into your business model brings about additional benefits that extend beyond the one-on-one coaching relationship.

These include:

- Potential for increasing your one-on-one client rooster while maximizing your audience reach

- Enhanced learning and retention through discussion and exploration

- Diverse perspectives that refine understanding

- Feedback from multiple members of the group

- Accountability, social support and the freedom to take risks within a safe space

- Opportunity for the individual to develop their own voice and perspective in relation to peers

When you work individually with someone, it's easy to build a safe, courageous space through which transformation happens. However, the same space can be constructed within a group or team environment. The difference in this setting is that change is facilitated both by you and through the interactions of the group members.

There is a unique and powerful phenomenon at play when people get together around a common end goal or desired result. As the coach, you are the catalyst for change. The group members provide extra inspiration and support for each other in the process (and at times even for you). In addition, if you are working within a team environment, the group process allows you to be in the midst of the team and "their process."

This type of coaching is attractive to some for its ability to generate increased revenue. Even more attractive is the free time it creates between engagements. Though the session planning is a little different in comparison to a one-on-one session, the time required to do so isn't that much greater. Let's take a deeper look at the different ways coaches work with groups of clients.

Mastermind groups

At the top end of the financial scale, you have Mastermind Groups. These are often as small as three to six people and, for a few famous coaches, twenty to one hundred people. Masterminds appeal to clients for the personal attention they receive from both the coach and the other members of the group.

In addition to accomplishing their goals, your clients build relationships and grow their networks within a Mastermind session. This is a critical selling point. Plus, research suggests results are exponentially greater within a group setting (more on how and why coming up when we talk about community).

Masterminds are unique in that you as the coach intentionally assemble smaller groups of select people and charge top dollar for exclusivity. Each group member's own experience and expertise adds value to the coaching process, which not only multiplies your impact but allows for others to grow their network.

Coaching workshops

Workshops often range from half-day, full-day or multi-day events where participants engage in intensive discussions, activities and coaching around a particular subject or desired transformation. Depending on your niche, you could offer your next workshop on a wide variety of topics ranging from health and wellness or spiritual path-finding to life and career direction.

In Dr. Lori Bisbey's workshop, "Light Your Fire," she educates and coaches couples in rekindling marital intimacy. Not only does she help her clients put romance back on the front burner, she is also building a community of happily married couples who remain friends long after her workshops.

Ryan Murtfeldt of Two River's Coaching is another example. As a music teacher, he offers half-day workshops called "Teach and Flourish." Through these sessions, he helps teachers make a positive difference in their lives while helping their students do the same. Ryan builds community around the tough topics of self-care in the education industry, exploring the challenges of working inside the educational system and the stress and struggle of providing the best for their students.

Coaching retreats

Retreats are a variation of the workshop. They are typically held in locations that are out of town for most participants. This allows them to unwind and disconnect from their busy lives. Kind of like a working vacation, but the only thing they have to work on is themselves. That is unless your focus in business coaching! There are a wide variety of retreat centers where you and your guests are taken care of by staff, allowing you to focus solely on your coaching and workshop attendees.

In these scenarios, it's not uncommon for coaches to rent or reserve space from retreat centers, hotels, Airbnb or other locations that cater to this type of packaged retreat. Massages and spas can be part of the package. So too might trips into the Amazon rainforest or NYC nightlife. Get creative. If you are coaching around finding inner peace, a lakeside resort in Guatemala might be the perfect setting. If you specialize in developing artistic performance, you might plan a retreat that coincides with a Shakespeare festival.

Nicole Gnutzman of Soul Scape Coaching, is a great example. She is a former corporate executive and yogi who immerses herself and her participants in the high altitude of Lake Atitlán in Guatemala. There she partners with others to offer yoga, live music, dream circles and

Mayan ceremonies to a group of eager seekers ready to connect to their soul's journey in a deep nature experience.

Team coaching

Group coaching tends to form around specific topics or desired outcomes, for example stress reduction or intuitive listening. Team coaching works with an already formed "team" of individuals. Your job here is to support the team to develop as a cohesive unit around goals or objectives typically set by their employers. It's worth noting that some companies include the team in the design process. These companies recognize that employees are more amenable to change when they are personally invested in shaping the outcome of the process.

Depending on the company, the team leader or other stakeholders may or may not be included in the coaching process. However, I would highly recommend identifying someone or a small group of people internally who will be responsible for sustaining the changes and holding the rest of the team accountable after you are long gone.

Large group coaching

Groups can include larger numbers of people. Some may debate whether this is really coaching, viewing it instead as more akin to facilitation or education. Yet such an opportunity allows you to share valuable content with dozens to hundreds of people at once in a workshop setting or corporate event. How closely it conforms to our definition of coaching is up to you.

One way to personalize this type of setting is to coach a few people in a "hot seat" from the stage. You walk your selected few through the process while encouraging and engaging the entire audience to absorb and learn through the shared experience.

The key is audience engagement and participation. This is what leads your group toward development and growth. Simply bombarding them with a PowerPoint presentation and slide after slide of information is not coaching.

The power of community

Once again, we find ourselves at the center of exponential results. As I mentioned in the section about Masterminds, the power of a group setting is undeniable. And now there's proof.

Let's say you're leading a group of twenty-four men and women in a thirty-day health challenge centered on weight loss. Each week you conduct your group session and several of your attendees are high-achievers. As each participant shares the results of your coaching in relation to her experience, these individuals are setting a trend for success. In short, they become your champions in the room. This motivates the others while simultaneously promoting the success of your process – they make your work shine and motivate others along the way!

In addition to motivation and inspiration, the community setting also offers another critical type of value to the participant: deeper understanding. Shared experiences enrich our sense of understanding and perspective, especially when facing significant challenges.

An interesting study published in the *European Journal of Social Psychology* reported "value in extending the practice of individual goal setting to the group level."[1] Evidence suggests that "when a group itself plays some role in setting goals this can lead to enhanced performance relative to conditions in which goals are imposed by an external source," according to the study.

With data extracted from two different experiments conducted uniquely for this study, "findings point to the fact that although participative group goal setting is unlikely to deliver across-the-board benefits for performance, its benefits may become apparent (and may be especially welcome) under conditions where the challenges that a group faces are formidable."

In other words, the greater the task, the more beneficial it is to leverage the strengths of each individual in a group.

Other considerations

The beauty of group coaching programs and workshops is that you can help a larger number of people in less time. You can also offer lower prices per individual yet still generate the income you are worth. This is a real benefit if you are serving a client base that may not be able to afford your individual session rates.

Running groups is also a highly effective way to leverage your time for maximum financial return. The time you'll put into a ten-person workshop or program will be far less than the effort required for ten individual clients,

1 Haslam, S. Alexander, Jürgen Wegge, and Tom Postmes. 2009. "Are we on a learning curve or a treadmill? The benefits of partici-pative group goal setting become apparent as tasks become increas-ingly challenging over time." *European Journal of Social Psychology* 39: 430-446.

though each setting has its own intrinsic value. But it also requires enhanced coaching and group facilitation skills to ensure everyone gets what they expect (then spreads the word about their experience with you).

If running workshops or group coaching programs is for you, you'll want to gain skills in group leadership, and facilitation. Individual skill sets often include time management, conflict management, effective presentation of information, and of course, professional coach skills that ensure everyone in the room receives the same level of value, feels included, and enjoys the experience.

Something else to consider is what works best for your clients. This may be a mixture of one-on-one coaching with regular group coaching to provide exposure to alternative points of view. In particular, certain topics are more conducive to group work than others – life coaching is one popular example. Depending on the topic, gender preferences may also be a factor.

Although not commonly the case, there is the potential for setbacks in a group setting. Sometimes people feel less inclined to participate in larger groups, stalling their own progress as they give way to those with naturally more dominant personalities. As introverts or extroverts, we all have our comfort level. Balancing the two personality types in a group setting to ensure everyone walks away with their goals met presents both the challenge and often the shortcoming of this coaching model.

And finally, it can be hard to find physical space for a large group without advance notice. If you plan on offering breakout sessions, this will be especially important. Procure your location early then market yourself well to fill the seats. Don't forget the food, or at least the coffee/

tea/juice bar. If at all possible, make sure you have a plan for catering or pick a location with cafés or restaurants within walkable distance.

Groups are definitely a lot of fun. And the community they produce is amazing! Although they aren't for everyone, hosting one or two a year can substantially boost your income. Which brings me to your third option.

Leverage your brilliance through passive income

How you choose to work with clients and the type of change you want to make have a tremendous impact on the delivery method you pursue. This is exponentially true of the third coaching option – one in which you have the potential to impact millions with your experience and unique point of view: coaching products and programs.

Imagine taking the wisdom, processes, and experience you've gathered by coaching individuals and running workshops then repackaging it for a global audience. Online coaching products allow you to leverage your wisdom by serving your ideal clients through video and audio tutorials, coaching tool kits, books, lectures and seminars, and electronic materials.

The options are unlimited. These passive income streams enable you to tap directly into your unique value, monetizing it for the broadest possible audience. This process represents the gateway to extra income and the freedom that goes along with it. By using the cost-effective and automated simplicity of an online course, you can sell these goods and services to a limitless range of individuals through an e-commerce outlet that never closes.

Coaching products

Coaching products allow people to work at their own pace and on their own time. They offer you more exposure, access to the global marketplace, and streams of income that work for you 24/7. For your clients, they provide affordable access to your wisdom and work.

Although the creation of content can require considerable amounts of time, effort and expense to develop, the return on your investment can be well worth it. Plus, once the initial effort is complete, the only time or monetary investment that remains is to market it. And since your coaching product literally just sits out there in the global marketplace, you can potentially make money 365 days a year.

The ultimate positioning tool, your coaching products also legitimize you as a thought-leader and changemaker. As the owner of intellectual property, you can quickly become the authority of your chosen niche. They also serve as a calling card or invitation to your ideal clients, inviting them to come explore your work with you.

While electronic resources are on the rise, coaching products aren't limited to e-books, online courses, apps, and other tools in the digital format. They can just as easily be a physical product like cards, games, workbooks, hardback books, or anything else that is cost-effective to manufacture and produce and represents your brand.

Coaching programs

In comparison, a coaching program often includes digital on-demand content supported with personal interactions that vary from in-person meetings and online connections through Facebook or other private online groups to live calls or videoconferencing.

Digital coaching

E-mail coaching and digital coaching websites have grown in popularity. Some coaches offer e-mail coaching as a standalone service or supplement to weekly-scheduled sessions. E-mail and text-based interactions are definitely in line with current communication preferences (especially among younger clients).

Keep in mind that working via e-mail has drawbacks due to the limitations of text-based communication. If anything, I recommend using it as a supplement to live in-person sessions, whether conducted in the same physical location or through a video conference platform.

Create your ideal coaching business model

As you create your ideal business model, know which options work best for you and your clients. If you consider yourself an introvert or are highly sensitive, you might work one-on-one out of personal preference. If the topics you coach around warrant the need for maximum privacy, this may also necessitate one-on-one sessions, or at the very least small groups with a guarantee of confidentiality from all members.

Or maybe, like many of us, you simply get a "charge" from one-on-one interaction, witnessing the changes you help make in real life. If that sounds like a comfortable fit, you may benefit from starting the way I did.

Private clients can be worth anywhere from $20,000 to $100,000 for celebrity or highly-regarded coaches like Marshall Goldsmith and Tony Robbins. That makes this coaching method just as valuable as working with larger numbers of people. On the whole, these numbers are often obtained by coaches who have specialized (and marketed themselves) and earned a reputation with their good work.

If you are a content creator and love creating products, your model might center on passive income as the bulk of your revenue stream. Add in a once-a-year private retreat at a fun resort for the tribe you've built through product sales (a.k.a. your Facebook community), and you have the foundation of a business you love – a business that seems like little work and all play.

If you are more interested in the number of lives changed than dollars earned, consider ways to create affordable large-scale workshops, programs and online products. Tony Robbins is a master at this. He runs weekend workshops in conference centers and auditoriums with thousands of people in a single session.

Whatever you decide for your business model, build your skills through a one-on-one practice. Start by collecting a variety of powerful testimonials then launch your group program or workshops. You'll learn valuable lessons around how best to serve and transform your clients' lives. More importantly, you'll develop the skills and capacity to reliably generate these results time and time again within a limitless range of personal and professional applications.

And there's more...

Many coaches go on to become authors, speakers, teachers, and subject matter experts because of the experience and expertise they acquire through coaching. They didn't start up as experts, but rather leveraged their experience and learned the rest as they went along.

No matter which avenue you pursue, it's critical to have a business plan that maximizes your time, money and energy. Pay attention to the life you wish to create through your business. It's one of the many gifts of being your own boss. Your time is a precious commodity, as is the quality of your life.

Being a coach is by far one of the most creative and innovative careers available. It offers a wide variety of options ranging from who you want to coach and how you want to coach them to how you'll earn your money (working for others or yourself). Many coaches have also achieved tremendous success by creating elaborate business models, speaking, writing, and developing programs in addition to their individual and group work.

The road is endless and abundant with options. And those who travel the road with their clients long enough to understand their needs will have the inner edge necessary to generate results, as well as passive income. Today's most successful, renowned coaches once stood where you are standing right now. So start where you are and build as you go!

Chapter review and coming attractions

By now you should recognize that becoming a coach isn't limited to working one-on-one or in-person with your ideal clients.

Using a combination of these delivery methods, you can create your ideal business model and ensure you have the greatest impact possible on those you desire to serve, not to mention the income to make it possible.

Next Up: We'll take an in-depth look at the ICF credential, including what it is, how each of the levels differ, what's required for each, and the doors you can expect each to open. You'll also learn how to compare the different training options available to you, and discover one in particular you should probably avoid.

~ *In Your Journal* ~

- Pause for a moment. Do you feel as excited as I do about all your options? Or do your feel a little overwhelmed with too many options? Rest assured that you have the ultimate choice in how you offer your services.

- With that in mind, what feels right for you? Do you prefer to work one-on-one? With groups? Masterminds? Retreats? Digital coaching?

- If you are most interested in coaching groups, imagine yourself at the front of the room, circled by a group of delighted clients. Or if your style leans more toward working online, imagine the laptop lifestyle you could have with coaching. Whatever you desire, give yourself the "felt" experience of having it as your reality by envisioning your future as if it was already here. Your mind is a powerful tool to step into your future. Go explore.

~7~

Credibility Counts: Rise above and get discovered

Competition is a fact of life. With the broad reach of the Internet, your audience is limitless. But you're also competing with coaches around the world. Leverage the power of a coach credential to stand out in a crowded marketplace.

One of the easiest ways to position yourself above others is with a credential conferred by the world's most widely recognized organization of professionally trained coaches, the International Coach Federation, or ICF for short. When you earn an ICF credential, you are signifying to prospective clients and employers that you have completed standardized requirements pertaining not just to the latest techniques, but also time-tested best practices. A credential elevates your expertise and profile from an amateur to an esteemed professional.

Consider this: seventy-seven percent of coach practitioners reported that clients expect them to be certified or credentialed, according to the 2016 ICF Global Coaching Study. As the profession matures, the general public is growing wiser, with expectations rising in tandem.

This is further reflected in legislation. In Oregon, senators recently attempted to license coaching and similar professions. Though you may not live in Oregon, these movements have a tendency to spread. Once one state government finds success in licensing a product or profession, it's that much easier for those that follow suit.

Stop and think for a minute. If you want to practice as a doctor, nurse, therapist or even a CPA, you'll have to earn board certification or qualify for a state board license respectively. Such credentials signify the professionalism and commitment of the individuals involved. Why should the profession of coaching be exempt from the same level of requirement?

What is the International Coach Federation (ICF)?

Much like an Ivy League university, the International Coach Federation, or ICF, is the premiere organization for earning your coaching credential. As a non-profit, they are dedicated to industry standards related to the practice of coaching and currently boast 28,000 members in 138 countries.

The ICF is recognized throughout the world for its:

- Coaching core competencies
- Professional code of ethics and standards
- Internationally-recognized coach credentialing program
- Broad collection of materials and ongoing studies related to coaching research
- Accreditation of coach training institutes
- Professional / self-regulatory oversight

With a history that dates back to 1995, the ICF is uniquely dedicated to the advancement of the coaching profession. They ensure the quality, reliability and effectiveness of coaching services around the world through high standards, independent certification, and the ongoing development of a global network of credentialed coaches who are required to uphold a strict code of ethics.

Their core purpose is to advance the art, science and practice of professional coaching. In keeping with this mission, the ICF offers the most globally-recognized, independent credentialing program available. It provides the vital core competencies that serve as a foundation for any coaching practice and is considered the "gold standard" for the profession.

As the coaching profession adapts itself into an ever-broader range of industries, from the arts and information technology (IT) to healthcare and financial services, the ICF functions similar to the Better Business Bureau in the

United States. They offer a reliable database of qualified coaches and coach training organizations. So much so, that the ICF's Credentialed Coach Finder is often the first stop for many prospective employers and coaching clients looking to match their specific needs with an individual coach's expertise.

The ICF envisions a future in which professional coaching will be an integral part of society, with its members representing the highest authority and integrity in this specialized career path.

Earning your ICF credential

Earning your ICF credential requires your commitment to a process that will separate you from other coaches. In just a few pages, I'll cover the specific requirements to earn your ICF credential.

The ICF currently offers three levels of credentialing for coaches:

- ACC – Associate Credentialed Coach
- PCC – Professional Credentialed Coach
- MCC – Master Credentialed Coach

Originally, the ICF started by offering the MCC level. But after extensive feedback about the duration it took to earn such an advanced status, they created two lower levels. The intention is that coaches will continue their professional development and proceed toward their PCC or MCC status while still possessing the capability to operate as a credentialed coach.

Difference between ICF credentials

Each ICF credential represents a different level of training, coaching experience and mentoring. The ACC level is akin to attending a two-year college. You emerge with a firm grasp of the fundamentals. The PCC is like earning an undergraduate degree. It represents your successful navigation of a full professional program, significant coaching experience, mentoring, and skill evaluations while specializing within the chosen area of your experience as a coach.

The MCC level represents your commitment to the profession with advanced trainings and thousands of hours of coaching experience. Most professional coaches train to become PCCs, initiating their credential process by initially earning their ACC and then either renewing their credential or moving up. How far you go and how quickly you advance is entirely up to you.

Credentialing requirements

To obtain your ICF credential, you must complete a set amount of coach specific training hours and ICF mentor coaching hours. These are obtained through your coach training program. Additionally, you'll have coaching experience and a Coach Knowledge Assessment (CKA).

Here's a snapshot of the requirements for each level.

Requirements for ACC, PCC and MCC Credentials			
	Associate Certified Coach (ACC) *For the Practiced Coach*	Professional Certified Coach (PCC) *For the Proven Coach*	Master Certified Coach (MCC) *For the Expert Coach*
Coach Specific Training (Hours Completed)	60+	125+	200+
Client Coach Experience Required (Hours Completed)	100+ hours (75 paid) of coaching experience with at least 8 clients	500+ hours (450 paid) of coaching experience with at least 25 clients	2,500+ hours (2,250 paid) of coaching experience with at least 35 clients
Mentor Coaching (Hours Completed)	10+	10+	10+
Coach Knowledge Assessment (CKA)	Yes	Yes	Yes

I'll be the first to admit: the numbers can be overwhelming – in particular those relating to service hours. But what you have to remember is that the bulk of your training and coaching practice hours are experiential. You won't be spending countless hours buried in books; you'll be learning in action.

Students have come to me and admitted they're intimidated by the requirements, without even realizing what they entail. Let's take a quick look at the line items, and what you can expect to gain from each.

Coach Specific Training

This is your classroom instruction. In this phase, you'll be learning the skills, tools, research and knowledge involved with becoming a coach. For those who pursue an ICF credential, this takes shape in the ICF's 11 Core Competencies where you are trained on the ICF's ethics, standards and best practices.[1] These include:

A. Setting the Foundation

1. Meeting Ethical Guidelines and Professional Standards—Understanding of coaching ethics and standards and ability to apply them appropriately in all coaching situations.

- Understands and exhibits in own behaviors the ICF Code of Ethics (see Code, Part III of ICF Code of Ethics).

- Understands and follows all ICF Ethical Guidelines.

- Clearly communicates the distinctions between coaching, consulting, psychotherapy and other support professions.

- Refers client to another support professional as needed, knowing when this is needed and the available resources.

2. Establishing the Coaching Agreement—Ability to understand what is required in the specific coaching interaction and to come to agreement with the prospective and new client about the coaching process and relationship.

---

1 International Coach Federation. n.d. "Core Competencies." *Core Competencies*. Accessed April 4, 2018. https://coachfederation.org/core-competencies.

- Understands and effectively discusses with the client the guidelines and specific parameters of the coaching relationship (e.g., logistics, fees, scheduling, inclusion of others if appropriate).

- Reaches agreement about what is appropriate in the relationship and what is not, what is and is not being offered, and about the client's and coach's responsibilities.

- Determines whether there is an effective match between his/her coaching method and the needs of the prospective client.

B. Co-Creating the Relationship

3. Establishing Trust and Intimacy with the Client— Ability to create a safe, supportive environment that produces ongoing mutual respect and trust.

1. Shows genuine concern for the client's welfare and future.

2. Continuously demonstrates personal integrity, honesty and sincerity.

3. Establishes clear agreements and keeps promises.

4. Demonstrates respect for client's perceptions, learning style, personal being.

5. Provides ongoing support for and champions new behaviors and actions, including those involving risk-taking and fear of failure.

6. Asks permission to coach client in sensitive, new areas.

4. Coaching Presence—Ability to be fully conscious and create spontaneous relationship with the client, employing a style that is open, flexible and confident.

1. Is present and flexible during the coaching process, dancing in the moment.

2. Accesses own intuition and trusts one's inner knowing—"goes with the gut."

3. Is open to not knowing and takes risks.

4. Sees many ways to work with the client and chooses in the moment what is most effective.

5. Uses humor effectively to create lightness and energy.

6. Confidently shifts perspectives and experiments with new possibilities for own action.

7. Demonstrates confidence in working with strong emotions and can self-manage and not be overpowered or enmeshed by client's emotions.

C. Communicating Effectively

5. Active Listening—Ability to focus completely on what the client is saying and is not saying, to understand the meaning of what is said in the context of the client's desires, and to support client self-expression.

1. Attends to the client and the client's agenda and not to the coach's agenda for the client.

2. Hears the client's concerns, goals, values and beliefs about what is and is not possible.

3. Distinguishes between the words, the tone of voice, and the body language.

4. Summarizes, paraphrases, reiterates, and mirrors back what client has said to ensure clarity and understanding.

5. Encourages, accepts, explores and reinforces the client's expression of feelings, perceptions, concerns, beliefs, suggestions, etc.

6. Integrates and builds on client's ideas and suggestions.

7. "Bottom-lines" or understands the essence of the client's communication and helps the client get there rather than engaging in long, descriptive stories.

8. Allows the client to vent or "clear" the situation without judgment or attachment in order to move on to next steps.

6. Powerful Questioning—Ability to ask questions that reveal the information needed for maximum benefit to the coaching relationship and the client.

1. Asks questions that reflect active listening and an understanding of the client's perspective.

2. Asks questions that evoke discovery, insight, commitment or action (e.g., those that challenge the client's assumptions).

3. Asks open-ended questions that create greater clarity, possibility or new learning.

4. Asks questions that move the client toward what they desire, not questions that ask for the client to justify or look backward.

7. Direct Communication—Ability to communicate effectively during coaching sessions, and to use language that has the greatest positive impact on the client.

1. Is clear, articulate and direct in sharing and providing feedback.

2. Reframes and articulates to help the client understand from another perspective what he/she wants or is uncertain about.

3. Clearly states coaching objectives, meeting agenda, and purpose of techniques or exercises.

4. Uses language appropriate and respectful to the client (e.g., non-sexist, non-racist, non-technical, non-jargon).

5. Uses metaphor and analogy to help to illustrate a point or paint a verbal picture.

D. Facilitating Learning and Results

8. Creating Awareness—Ability to integrate and accurately evaluate multiple sources of information and to make interpretations that help the client to gain awareness and thereby achieve agreed-upon results.

1. Goes beyond what is said in assessing client's concerns, not getting hooked by the client's description.

2. Invokes inquiry for greater understanding, awareness, and clarity.

3. Identifies for the client his/her underlying concerns; typical and fixed ways of

perceiving himself/herself and the world; differences between the facts and the interpretation; and disparities between thoughts, feelings, and action.

4. Helps clients to discover for themselves the new thoughts, beliefs, perceptions, emotions, moods, etc. that strengthen their ability to take action and achieve what is important to them.

5. Communicates broader perspectives to clients and inspires commitment to shift their viewpoints and find new possibilities for action.

6. Helps clients to see the different, interrelated factors that affect them and their behaviors (e.g., thoughts, emotions, body, and background).

7. Expresses insights to clients in ways that are useful and meaningful for the client.

8. Identifies major strengths vs. major areas for learning and growth, and what is most important to address during coaching.

9. Asks the client to distinguish between trivial and significant issues, situational vs. recurring behaviors, when detecting a separation between what is being stated and what is being done.

9. Designing Actions—Ability to create with the client opportunities for ongoing learning, during coaching and in work/life situations, and for taking new actions that will most effectively lead to agreed-upon coaching results.

1. Brainstorms and assists the client to define actions that will enable the client to demonstrate, practice, and deepen new learning.

2. Helps the client to focus on and systematically explore specific concerns and opportunities that are central to agreed-upon coaching goals.

3. Engages the client to explore alternative ideas and solutions, to evaluate options, and to make related decisions.

4. Promotes active experimentation and self-discovery, where the client applies what has been discussed and learned during sessions immediately afterward in his/her work or life setting.

5. Celebrates client successes and capabilities for future growth.

6. Challenges client's assumptions and perspectives to provoke new ideas and find new possibilities for action.

7. Advocates or brings forward points of view that are aligned with client goals and, without attachment, engages the client to consider them.

8. Helps the client "Do It Now" during the coaching session, providing immediate support.

9. Encourages stretches and challenges but also a comfortable pace of learning.

10. Planning and Goal Setting—Ability to develop and maintain an effective coaching plan with the client.

1. Consolidates collected information and establishes a coaching plan and development goals with the client that address concerns and major areas for learning and development.

2. Creates a plan with results that are attainable, measurable, specific, and have target dates.

3. Makes plan adjustments as warranted by the coaching process and by changes in the situation.

4. Helps the client identify and access different resources for learning (e.g., books, other professionals).

5. Identifies and targets early successes that are important to the client.

11. Managing Progress and Accountability—Ability to hold attention on what is important for the client, and to leave responsibility with the client to take action.

1. Clearly requests of the client actions that will move the client toward his/her stated goals.

2. Demonstrates follow-through by asking the client about those actions that the client committed to during the previous session(s).

3. Acknowledges the client for what they have done, not done, learned or become aware of since the previous coaching session(s).

4. Effectively prepares, organizes, and reviews with client information obtained during sessions.

5. Keeps the client on track between sessions by holding attention on the coaching plan and outcomes, agreed-upon courses of action, and topics for future session(s).

6. Focuses on the coaching plan but is also open to adjusting behaviors and actions based on the coaching process and shifts in direction during sessions.

7. Is able to move back and forth between the big picture of where the client is heading, setting a context for what is being discussed and where the client wishes to go.

8. Promotes client's self-discipline and holds the client accountable for what they say they are going to do, for the results of an intended action, or for a specific plan with related time frames.

9. Develops the client's ability to make decisions, address key concerns, and develop himself/herself (to get feedback, to determine priorities and set the pace of learning, to reflect on and learn from experiences).

10. Positively confronts the client with the fact that he/she did not take agreed-upon actions.

Client Coach Experience

Your Client Coach Experience is the hours you spend professionally coaching another person or group. This on-the-job training can be comprised of any variety of coaching clients, including individuals or groups (of no more than fifteen people), as well as internal or third-party clients.

To qualify for credit, a coaching hour must be sixty minutes in length and be in service to a client who has hired you specifically for your coaching expertise. So if someone calls you to facilitate a meeting, teach a class, or offer consulting, this does not count toward your ICF credential.

There may also be cases when a full hour is too long for either you and your client. These shorter sessions count as partial client coaching hours. For example, a thirty-minute session (also quite common) counts as .5 toward your total of client coaching hours.

Additionally, seventy-five percent of your coaching practice needs to be paid hours. This requirement is often the one that enables coaching students to pay for the cost of their training and even have some left over for a business startup. It's also worth noting that "payment" can be received monetarily or in the barter of goods or services. This can even include coaching in exchange for coaching.

The one catch here is that any coaching you perform inside of the coach specific training portion of your program does not count toward your client coaching tally. Only those hours outside of class. And per changes instituted in 2016, client coach experience hours only begin to accumulate after you begin your coach training. Any coaching you complete before starting your coach training program, though excellent practice, cannot be applied to a credential.

Who counts as a client?

This is another area of freedom many coaching students enjoy. During training, the ICF allows you to coach those types of clients you aspire to serve as a professional coach. Though the variations are limitless, these are often represented by five primary groups:

Individuals: Frequently the most popular of the five options, coaching individuals allows you to get your feet wet almost immediately. The hours you log coaching individuals within your chosen niche count toward your total requirement of client coach experience while simultaneously igniting the spark that will soon be your unique impact on the world.

Peer to peer: As mentioned earlier, this is the exchange of coaching between two peer coaches. This is another popular way for new coaches to hone their skills in a safe environment that, for some, offers considerably less stress than coaching a "real" client. Remember though, these hours only count when conducted outside your coach training courses. Peer to peer coaching often takes place in the classroom, but these hours cannot be applied to your client coach experience tally.

Groups: This is identical to the groups you will one day offer within your own business or third-party setting. To qualify for client coach experience, you must have the group participants establish their own agenda; and the session must be interactive. In other words, there must be a coaching exchange between you and your participants. This obviously disqualifies seminars, presentations and other gatherings in which you simply offer an established curriculum to a group of people. Also, if you coach a group of fifteen people for three hours, this is still recorded as only three hours of coaching experience.

Internal Coaching: Many people begin coach training while working for someone else. It's a fantastic way to get started. Many companies (larger organizations in particular) may even offer reimbursement as part of an employee development initiative. In exchange, you are often expected to use your coaching skills as part of your regular employment.

Third-Party Coaching: In this scenario, you are employed within a business, non-profit or other organization and contracted to coach select individuals or groups. Your hours are logged the same way they would be for standard coaching clients. But instead of receiving payment from these clients individually, you are paid for your work by the hiring organization.

ICF Mentor Coaching

In addition to your coach training and practical experience, you'll work with an ICF mentor coach. Your coach offers constructive coaching and feedback through an ongoing dialog. They provide notes on your strengths and areas in which you stand to improve your process. Their feedback is based on observed coaching sessions both live and recorded, if applicable. If this sounds intimidating, don't stress. The goal is to fine-tune your process. This ensures you are not only delivering the results your clients expect but doing so in a consistent and reliable way reflective of ICF Core competencies and ethics.

The ICF requires you to partner with a mentor coach for at least three months and a total of ten hours minimum. Your mentor coach is also required to hold a credential equal to or greater than the one you are pursuing.

There are a few additional requirements to be aware of when working with your ICF mentor coach:

- **Individual and group coaching** – If you are interested in jumping right into group coaching, know that the ICF requires you to have a minimum of three hours (out of the total ten) as one-on-one mentor coaching. The remaining seven hours can be filled by group coaching.

- **Documentation** – When filling out your credential application, you'll need to include your mentor coach's name, email, credential level, start and end date of your mentor coaching relationship, and the total hours you worked with the mentor (or mentors if you work with more than one). No other documentation is required. But if contacted, your mentor coach may be asked to verify the information you provide.

It's worth noting that when you attend an ICF Accredited Coach Training Program (ACTP), your mentoring hours are typically included in your program. For example, Coach Training World's ICF programs are all-inclusive. But that's not always the case. Check to see if your ICF mentor coaching hours incur an additional (and sometimes hidden) cost with any other schools you consider.

The ICF considers mentor coaching to be "vital to the development and growth of the individual seeking an ICF Credential." I couldn't agree more. When working with a mentor coach, your skills can grow exponentially from the individualized support you'll receive.

Coach Knowledge Assessment (CKA)

Yes, there's a test. But again, don't stress. When you apply for your ICF credential, you'll have to complete what's known as a Coach Knowledge Assessment (CKA). The questions are all multiple-choice (one hundred fifty-five of them in all) and must be completed within three hours. Questions are based on the ICF definition of coaching, eleven Core Competencies, and the Code of Ethics with varying difficulty levels. You can also expect a certain number of questions on specific concepts or skills as well as unique scenarios.

A passing score of seventy percent is required. On the off-chance you don't pass, you can opt to retake a different version of the test. The good news is, you only have to pass the test once. For example, you'll take it when you work toward your ACC credential, but not again if you pursue a PCC or MCC credential.

How long does it take to earn a credential?

This all depends on how much time you devote. You can receive your training and mentoring over a period of just a few months. But you can't start recording your coaching practicum hours until you officially start your first class. For this reason, most people getting to the PCC level find it takes them six to twenty-four months. That's why many students apply for their ACC in the interim. Plus, during that time, they aren't just sitting around earning their credential. They are building their business and clientele.

Why earn a credential?

As of October 2017, there are 14,039 Associate Certified Coaches (ACC), 8,194 Professional Certified Coaches (PCC), and 831 Master Certified Coaches (MCC). Yours truly is proud to be one among the latter. These coaches have gone on to successfully launch their own business, partner up with others, or pursue coaching within a corporate setting.

Yes, there's only one you. Only you can use your unique brilliance to make your chosen impact in the world. But without a credential, it's going to be extremely difficult to position yourself as a "professional" coach.

Cornerstone of trust

Credentials denote trust. They demonstrate your competence and are one of the first testaments to your reputation. Personal positioning aside, earning your ICF credential also contributes to the global image of professional coaching.

In addition, the *2017 ICF Global Consumer Awareness Study* found that eighty-three percent of clients who had previous experience with coaching "stated it was either important or very important that their coach has a certification/credential. Interestingly, those who had no experience of coaching also felt coaching certifications/ credentials were important, although the proportion of respondents stating certifications/credentials were either important or very important was somewhat smaller (76%)."[2]

2 International Coach Federation. *2017 ICF Global Consumer Awareness Study*. Research. Accessed April 4, 2018. https://coachfederation.org/research/consumer-awareness-study.

In today's world of quick, easy solutions, where anyone can launch a website and give themselves any title they dream up, an ICF credential demonstrates your commitment to the profession.

Increased income

An ICF credential symbolizes your familiarity with the best practices and code of ethics for our profession. That particular feather in your cap has real monetary value. According to information published in the *2016 ICF Global Coaching Study*, "coaches who hold a credential from a professional coaching association report higher annual revenue from coaching than their peers without a credential."[3]

There is substantial and increasing value between credentialing levels (ACC, PCC and MCC). First, there is a notable increase in the fees you can command. Depending on your level of certification and area of focus, coaches have reported anywhere from $125 to $500 an hour for government and private sector contracts.

The reason for this sizable gap is the difference in capacity between the three levels of certification. You gain a significantly increased ability to assist your clients, both within your chosen niche and all other areas of their lives, when you complete advanced certifications.

---

3 International Coach Federation. *2016 ICF Global Coaching Study. Research*. Accessed April 4, 2018. https://coachfederation.org/research/global-coaching-study.

Competence and confidence

ition to the wide range of coaching knowledge and techniques they learn, credentialed coaches also walk away with something essential for success: confidence. You've completed the course work. You've worked side-by-side with a mentor coach, completing your practicum requirements. You know what you're doing. A credential is the fastest way to let others know it too."

Credential as part of a background check

As previously mentioned, it has become increasingly common for clients and employers to verify a coach's credential. This is especially true when applying for a bidding solicitation or request for proposal (RFP). Several graduates of Coach Training World have recently told me about standard job opportunities that require a credential. This will also be the case if you want to attend advanced workshops like Brené Brown's, The Daring Way.

When a prospective employer verifies your credential, they are essentially looking for three things. These are as much a testament to the coach training program you attended as they are evidence of your ability. In short, your credential tells others:

- You successfully completed a professional coaching practicum

- You received supervised, professional mentoring by a seasoned coach, developing your skills to an established standard of excellence

- You attended a reputable, vetted coach training school

As coaches, we all start somewhere. But when you start inside a professionally accredited training institute such as Coach Training World, you immediately begin learning through practice with supervision. In more than two decades in this business, I can tell you with certainty: there is no faster way to solidify the tools and techniques of coaching than through experiential learning with an expert mentor by your side.

A credential:

- Reassures clients by establishing your credibility as a professional

- Demonstrates your adherence to established standards and code of ethics

- Testifies to your specific level of skill and personal knowledge

- Requires ongoing development (for renewal), further broadening your capability, proficiency and potential results

- Upholds the image of a "professional" coach

- Includes a one-of-a-kind marketing tool: an ICF logo you can use to advertise your specific credential, ACC, PCC or MCC

If you are serious about building and maintaining a well-respected, self-regulating coaching business, or maintaining a professional credential, you may want to obtain your ICF credential or a similar status through a reputable, ICF-accredited organization.

Coach training programs (watch your step!)

There's no easy way to have this next conversation: not all coach training schools are created equal. In the same way that anyone can add "coach" after their name, so too can that same person craft a quick coach training program and offer "certification." Unfortunately, these certifications are usually not recognized by anyone but that school – and sometimes not even then. This makes it challenging to know what school to attend.

Much like the credentialed process you'll follow as a coach trainee, coach training schools must also demonstrate their competency with curriculum standards and best practices. This guarantees consistency of practice among credentialed coaches. On behalf of your future as a change maker, I implore you to examine the distinctions between an accredited coach training program and one that isn't.

There are four coach training options:

1. ACTP (ICF Accredited Coach Training Program)
2. ACSTH (ICF Approved Coaching Specific Training Hours)
3. CCE (ICF Continuing Coaching Education)
4. Non-Accredited Schools

Accredited Coach Training Programs (ACTP)

Institutions who have earned the ICF Accredited Coach Training Program (ACTP) distinction are accredited, fully vetted, and maintain the highest standards for comprehensive instruction around the ICF's core competencies, code of ethics and definition of coaching. These standards require accredited schools to have a

Master Coach (MCC) as training director, ensuring you are learning from the best.

An ACTP training program is typically all-inclusive. It provides a minimum of sixty to two hundred hours of basic- to advanced-level coach specific training, your required ICF mentor coaching, as well as the opportunity to practice coaching with evaluations and an oral test.

One of the big perks of attending an ACTP program is that you receive mentoring by an ICF professional coach who holds at least a PCC certification. These individuals are frequently the best part of the program, according to many of our graduates. They offer insight and wisdom that simplify and elevate the process for those seeking their ICF credential. In many cases, these relationships continue well beyond the training requirements, with the mentor coach acting as a reliable sounding board and ongoing source of guidance.

Once you complete the full ACTP program, you'll possess the skills necessary to apply for the ICF's Professional Certified Coach credential (PCC) as well as the training hours to apply for ICF Global Membership. You can review the full list of application requirements for this program type of accreditation here: https://www. coachfederation.org/program.

Approved Coach Specific Training Hours (ACSTH)

This a' la carte option may or may not qualify as a full coach training program depending on the course content. An ACSTH program includes at least thirty hours of coach-specific training centered on the ICF's Core Competencies and observed coaching sessions by a qualified, credentialed coach. Students who attend an

ACSTH program are required to submit performance evaluations (two audio recordings and written transcripts of coaching sessions to be uploaded with your ICF application). In addition, the application fees are nearly double, as is the turn-around time for the credentialing process.

Continuing Coach Education (CCE)

This option is used by thousands of coaches every year to renew their ICF credential. These are the courses that allow you to deepen and strengthen your coaching capacity and knowledge. Through CCEs, many coaches have discovered a new aspect of their calling, broadening their service offerings to areas they hadn't previously considered but were well suited to as a result of experience and passion.

Continuing Coach Education is exactly that – designed for those who have already completed basic training and hold at least an ACC. Though they may appear in the roster of a full coach training program, they are not a program in and of themselves.

Non-accredited schools

Unless you've skipped around the book up to this point, what I'm going to say next should come as no surprise: non-accredited schools are a risky proposition. Again, as someone who has been on the receiving end of these types of trainings, I know how it feels to walk in eager to learn something new and emerge half a day later with nothing to show for it but a complimentary soda and a head full of someone else's origin story. And I don't even drink soda.

With these goals in mind, it's critical to choose a coach training program that is ICF accredited. Opting only for coach training programs that are fully accredited ensures you are going to receive the quality training, mentoring and support you need to succeed in the business of change.

Board Certified Coach (BCC)

While the primary focus of this chapter is on earning your credential from the ICF, there is another option to be aware of: Board Certified Coach (BCC). This proves especially useful for those who currently serve others as a therapist, counselor, social worker, psychologist or the like. In these instances, individuals who already operate at a professional level can add coaching into their toolkit while applying their academic work experience toward the credential.

If you think you may qualify for this option, you can earn a Board Certified Coach credential (BCC) through the Center for Credentialing Education (CCE). While this is a valid option for many, it's important to look at how you want to employ your coaching skills. If you are building into an existing business or career, this option might be just right for you. If you are looking at starting your own business and pursuing a global client base, the ICF credential might be a better option for you due to its status as the gold standard in our profession.

At CTW, we give you the option to pursue one or both of these credentials.

Chapter review and coming attractions

In this chapter, we learned the best way to rise above others in the coaching industry is to earn a credential. It provides an established curriculum and pathway to success while offering the surest way to a sound return on your time and financial investment. One of the easiest ways to do so as a coach is with a credential conferred by the world's most widely recognized organization of professionally trained coaches, the International Coach Federation (ICF). But not all coach training schools offer the same level of service. Take time to carefully evaluate the credentials each school holds and the programs they offer. The safest route to your credential is through a school that provides an Accredited Coach Training Program (ACTP).

Next Up: We'll explore your path moving forward. The beauty of professional coaching is there's no set path everyone must follow. The journey is unique for each of us. Not only does this broaden the possibility of your success (monetizing your brilliance), it also ensures the success of your future clients (because no one can do what you do like you!). In these final chapters, I'll answer some of the most common questions students come to me with when they're feeling overwhelmed or are simply looking to clarify their direction.

~ In Your Journal ~

- Take into consideration all the ways having an ICF credential might help you succeed in the coaching profession.

- How might it add value and credibility to your reputation?

- Are you considering working in organizations or with people who will want to see a credential on your resume? Do you plan on enrolling in advanced trainings that require the ICF credential?

~8~

The Road Ahead: Treasured for who you are

Coaching isn't just a way to make a living. It's a way for you to make a life while contributing your best toward the betterment of those around you, and throughout the world.

You are truly unlimited. As a professional Whole Person Coach, you directly impact the lives of others. You not only address the issues your clients seek help with, you also empower them to carry this same drive toward positive change into other areas of their life. Word spreads. And when other people see the results of your efforts, your client roster grows. Add in the limitless reach of the Internet, and you now have potential to affect change in the lives of thousands or even millions of people across the world.

You also have the power to change the lives of those around you. Friends, family and your local community benefit from your skills and experience. Because coaching skills aren't just for coaching. They are life-success skills that belong to everyone.

As coaches, we naturally lean toward the betterment of others. But those changes would be impossible without first reshaping our own lives, realizing both our dreams and fullest potential.

When I started my first coaching business, I had no idea my decision to become a professional coach would lead me on such a life-changing path. People pay untold sums of money and spend decades to find their way home, back into the whole of who they are. Becoming a coach and starting my own coaching business gave me all of that and so much more.

Today I'm living a life fueled by my passions, one that is purposeful on many levels and prosperous in all aspects. The reward of shining my light in service to others is beyond words. I now have the freedom to be who I am and do what I want – a lifestyle each of us should enjoy. You included!

Learn to treasure yourself

Students and workshop participants often ask about the most important lessons I've learned. First among them is: treasure yourself. You might think this refers to money. But it's actually about so much more. Treasuring yourself is about prospering in all aspects of life. It begins when you reimagine your life and pursue what you are truly passionate about. It's about investing in yourself and your future. It's also about succeeding financially by getting paid what you're worth. Never forget: the support you offer as a changemaker is *truly* priceless.

The necessity of assigning this type of value to our lives is often the hardest lesson to trust. Too many of us are at odds with the validity of asking for what we truly want and being open to the possibilities that exist. And far more are lost in the daily grind while their precious life passes them by. As a result, many of us never reach our fullest potential because of the way in which fear holds us back, often beneath our radar.

But this doesn't have to be the case – and certainly not for you.

You are gifted, talented and deeply brilliant in your own unique way. Your capacity to grow and develop masterfully – inside and out – is truly without bounds. You are an incredible being, capable of anything. This is exponentially true when you surround yourself with empowering relationships that champion you toward your best. You are worthy of having a life you truly love, one that allows you to be who you are, at your very best.

At a moment in our history that finds us intentionally divided, isn't it time for people like you and me – who genuinely care about others – to do everything we can in our considerable power to lift those around us? Isn't it our responsibility to help those around us rise together rather than fall apart? Let it be so!

Your journey has begun

In the past couple hundred pages, I've given you a peek into the world of professional coaching. You've learned the importance of becoming professionally trained and earning the credibility of an ICF credential. The basics of creating your own unique niche and generating multiple streams of income as a coach have also been explained. And we've covered a few of the pitfalls to avoid. Yet, like life, there is more to learn.

You can do this.

You can become the successful coach you are meant to be. Here's how I know you can succeed. First and most importantly, you are not starting from scratch. As a coach, you'll employ the wisdom you've accumulated throughout your life. That means you are building upon your current experience and using coaching to facilitate the transformational results your clients will love you for. Technically, you are already in the fast lane, adding skills to become highly effective at influencing and motivating others. The real change coming up for you is the supplementation of your skills and capacity to impact others (and the world as a whole). If you are like many who are drawn to this profession, you've already been using some of the basic coaching skills. Now it's time to step up to the power tools!

The simple fact that you've made it through the entire book tells me something far more important: you are motivated by a calling that originates deep within. It guides what you may call your life's work, purpose or mission. Regardless of the exact term you apply, I am officially championing you to answer the call. It will lead you to places and feelings of pure joy, happiness and fulfilment. Every client who leaves you with a smile, a purpose, and an enhanced feeling of hope will serve as a reminder: you made the right choice.

And you are not alone. Had you come into the coaching profession decades ago, you would have found only a few of us. But coaching is here to stay; that means you have others to lean on for support and camaraderie.

Lastly, I know you have what it takes because you are a lifelong learner. You're committed to helping yourself be the best you can be. Adding more knowledge, skills and practical experience into your tool kit is an obvious next step. So when you do eventually click 'post' on a branded website with the title "coach" following your name, you'll be confident, prepared and well equipped to succeed.

Success is a choice

There are thousands of graduate success stories I could have chosen to share with you as this book closes. I chose Gary's because of the deep impact he's had on me.

While filming a testimonial video for Coach Training World (then operating as Baraka Institute: Leadership Development and Coach Training Center), we decided to ask some of the students to speak about coaching and their experience with the training they had received. During the filming process, I sat on the sidelines as the graduates shared their stories. All were powerful. Most centered on how they came into coaching and where it had taken their lives since.

But coaching isn't just about becoming a coach. The tools and methodology we choose shape our effectiveness in the world, often determining the scope of our impact.

Gary Warford is among the coaches who exemplify the successful navigation of this fact.

Gary began his professional career as a machinist. But he knew from an early age that he wanted to be involved with people. As a man of faith, he became a youth pastor, eventually working with teenagers in serval positions throughout the United States. With a passion for encouraging others, Gary wanted to help young people find the opportunities available to them by imparting wisdom gleaned from his experience: there's far more in life than what we initially see, regardless of our age. He then began working with adults in 2001 and discovered many of the same feelings he'd been dealing with in his youth ministry — people felt stuck in careers, lives or places in which they just weren't happy.

> *"As they would explore different parts of where they'd want to go, what they'd want to do, I found they loved the challenge," Gary says. "They loved the excitement of dreaming. As they would dream, they would come up with ideas that often went back to their childhood. 'Man, this is what I wanted to do as a kid' and 'why did I get away from it' [were] areas in which they would often challenge themselves."*

In a limited way, Gary was transitioning once again. This time, closer to his heart's desire. But it wasn't until he was fired from his job without notice after seven years that he answered his true calling. The sudden loss of employment left Gary in a funk. Eventually, a friend recommended he use a life coach. She had him dig down into his true values and rediscover what mattered most to him. Suddenly the answer became clear: Gary wanted to do what his coach was doing. Yet at the same time, he didn't necessarily want to work with people in a structured religious organization.

"At times, when I was a pastor, I felt limited on what I could do as far as helping people with personal development because they always wanted to tie a very strong religious, spiritual connection to it," Gary says. "And I think that is good. But that is not for everybody."

Gary began to explore the types of coaching available by comparing a variety of methodologies online. In his research, he found many coach training schools were geared more toward the cognitive aspect of personal development or would omit components he thought were important. Coach Training World stood out to Gary because of Whole Person Coaching, specifically its inclusiveness and the fact that it incorporates the wisdom taken from all aspects of an individual.

"There are many ways to connect and work with people," Gary says, "and we can't dismiss anything – physically, mentally, spiritually. We have to acknowledge all of those factors, because they really do meld together to help get us to a place where we are happy and are able to make the moves in life that we want to."

Unlike some however, Gary initially approached his training with some apprehension. Originally from the Midwest, he saw himself as having a narrow, "black and white" worldview, despite having lived in Oregon for nearly sixteen years. Admittedly, he was a little guarded when it came time to talk about his background in ministry. He viewed everyone in his cohort as being very different from him. But as he listened to everyone else tell their stories, Gary's perspective shifted. He realized how narrow his viewpoints had been, and that he'd missed a lot of opportunities for healthy, fun relationships as a result.

Likewise, Gary's cohort readily embraced him as a whole person. He was seen as far more than his role as a former pastor. The group grew deeply together through authenticity and the connections and empathy that evolved.

> *"I love my cohort," Gary says. "I'm still in contact with almost all of them. It really did become a bit of a family. For me, having had a major change in my career, having them there for support, for help, to challenge me, working together, dreaming big, has been huge – and we continue to do that in our conversations back and forth. So the relationship with the people I was [training] with, that was a key piece. And it continues on; and it's been ten years now."*

After completing his coach training in 2008, Gary began working with people who were navigating some form of recovery, from drugs and alcohol to gambling, porn and even shopping. This led him to expand his services to the field of corrections, providing help to those who were court mandated for anger management. He eventually created a coaching program that enabled those who were incarcerated to receive entrepreneurial training. Gary then added an additional certification as an educator from the Gottman Institute in Seattle and began working with couples alongside his wife Patty, a licensed psychologist. The husband and wife duo helped people by cultivating the realization that each partner in an intimate relationship brings something important. In the past few years, Gary has also added business owners to his list, coaching other leaders in how to be more effective through his Master Networks business.

Talk about impact!

With the tools and methodology of Whole Person Coaching in his tool kit, Gary contributes to the lives of everyone he sets his sights on. Through it all, his conviction has not wavered. Gary believes people are far more than just a job title or specific role. They're looking to get out of their labels and break free of who society tells them they should be. They want to figure out who they really are, and to find peace, comfort, excitement, and challenges in different areas of life. Gary is convinced this is only accomplished by harnessing the wisdom of the whole person. As a result, his clients not only leave happy, they are far more effective moving forward in their individual career path or role.

> *"There are a lot of opportunities to coach in different areas," Gary says. "Right now, my focus is people in business. What I have found with them is that they appreciate that we can talk business, but it's also important to take a look at the whole person. Who are they as an individual? They fill a role in a career or corporate America, but that's not the totality of who they are."*

In addition to the broad array of groups Gary helps, there's one more thing that really stands out. Gary recently got certified with his Goldendoodle, Dutton. This unique team travels around the Portland area working with an even more extensive range of those in need. Gary and Dutton's clients include:

- Individuals working through court-ordered anger management

- Lutheran Community Services Northwest and a group of two-year-olds who are low-income and have experienced trauma
- Students and faculty at the Oregon Institute of Technology

Though the coaching itself doesn't change, dogs bring a calmness and peace to the room, often providing an inroad Gary may have had to work harder to earn.

"People will sit and they'll talk to Dutton. They'll pet Dutton. But they will end up engaging with me," Gary says. "That's a whole different area I hadn't even thought of until Dutton was coming into the office and people would say, 'Hey, can Dutton come [into the session]?' We ended up getting certified so that we understand each other's body language, and he understands his job when we have a coaching client in. Dutton takes people to a different place. He makes us look really good!"

After hearing Gary's story, I realized my life's purpose entailed far more than I initially envisioned. I was deeply passionate about teaching people how to help others achieve their goals and dreams. But something was still tugging at me inside. Was there a way I could broaden my impact even further? Then it occurred to me: what about an army of changemakers – a group of likeminded souls committed to bringing more love, presence and kindness to the world?

That remains my mission to this day. I champion my students and clients to become highly influential leaders and holistic luminaries. In turn, they lead the way for others within their individual arenas and make their difference simply by being who they are at their absolute best.

Your turn...

As we close, I'd like to leave you with the central idea that inspired the penning of this book: coaching is not just for coaches; it is for the world and everyone in it. Through Whole Person Coaching, you can empower people to be the best possible version of themselves. This enhanced state, one that often embodies improvements across the board, sets people free. In turn, they affect those within their personal and professional lives. They see new possibilities. They discover the courage to act despite a lifetime of outdated patterns of belief. Or perhaps they simply offer a kind word and bit of encouragement to a friend, colleague or stranger they sit next to in a coffee shop. This spark was ignited by you. And in this way, your impact – your life – becomes truly exponential.

You picked up this book for a reason. Now that you've arrived at the end, how might becoming a coach change your life?

- New career?
- Enhanced relationships?
- Better decision-making skills?
- Community of like-minded people?
- Up-level your existing business?
- Reinvent your life?
- Influence others?
- Make your impact in the world?
- Generate a healthy income by doing what you love?
- Leave a legacy?

- Become a luminary and thought-leader in your own arena?

All are possible. As we learned right up front in Chapter 1: the benefits of a career or business in professional coaching are profound, limitless and grounded in your unique wisdom. Although you've reached the last few pages of this book, you've just cracked the cover on the story of your own journey. You stand at the beginning of a new life. A blank page, with infinite possibilities. What can you see on the horizon?

If you take away nothing else, know this: becoming a professional coach isn't just about you. It's about the lives you're going to change. There are so many people out there who need help – far outnumbering the luminaries like you and me.

Never forget: you have true value my friend. Your skills and experience comprise your unique brilliance. You can begin using that wisdom today to redirect, guide and enhance the course of your life, helping others.

You can do it!

But don't wait... Take your next steps right now!

Keep your momentum going by joining me in one of my virtual fireside conversations or upcoming webinars at: **www.coachtrainingworld.com**.

I'll expand on the concepts you've learned in this book so you can decide for yourself whether becoming a coach is your next step to a life, career and business you'll absolutely love.

Don't want to wait? You can reach us at 1-888-660-5588 or via email at info@coachtrainingworld.com

~9~

FAQs:
Change is coming.
You ready?

This book is dedicated to unveiling your roadmap to a career and life you'll absolutely love. My intention is to guide you toward the insights and proven strategies that allow you to become the successful coach you are meant to be. We've covered a lot of territory in the past eight chapters.

If you find yourself overwhelmed, take heart. Every coach who ever lived started out exactly where you are right now. That's the beauty of professional coaching. There's no set path everyone must follow without deviation; the journey is unique for each of us. Not only does this broaden the possibility of your success (monetizing your brilliance), it also ensures the success of your future clients (because no one can do what you do like you!)

You are now faced with a crucial decision. In many ways, it's one that holds the potential to be life-changing for both you and the lives you'll touch in your new career. So I wanted to share some of the frequently asked questions I've received over the years from coaches and prospective coaches alike. Again, you are not alone in your journey to become a professional coach. Everyone starts somewhere. By absorbing the lessons and knowledge of others, you can take your next small but significant steps toward becoming a successful coach in your area of passionate interests, expertise and experience.

For your convenience, questions are broken into groups as follows:

Transitioning into Coaching

- Realistically, what should I expect to invest (in time and money)?
- Is the marketplace overcrowded?
- Do I need to quit my job or leave my industry?
- How do I convince my partner, husband, wife or family to support me on this venture?
- How can I convince my employer to invest in my training?
- Who should *not* become a coach?
- What are other resources people use to pay their tuition?

Training & Credentialing

- How does online coach training work?
- How does coaching work with other modalities?
- How does coaching differ from therapy and consulting?
- What's the difference between the ICF and CCE?
- Do I need to pursue my ICF or BCC coaching credential?
- What is the ICF global network?

Starting Your Business

- How do I get clients?
- When can I quit my day job?
- What if I'm a new business owner?
- How long will it take to become profitable?
- What if I'm not famous or don't know very many people?
- How many products/programs do I need before I launch my coaching business?
- What if I can't devote forty hours a week to this?

Other Questions

- Does coaching really work?
- What if my life isn't perfect?

- What if someone in the coaching industry knows more than me?

- What other questions do you have?

Transitioning into Coaching

Realistically, what should I expect to invest (in time and money)?

If you pursue a full degree in coaching, such as a bachelor's, master's or PhD program in coaching, expect to pay anywhere between $9,400 and $32,400 per year. You will then be in school full-time from two to six years. At the upper limits of this path, you'll invest just under $200,000. Even just an average of the two at four years could cost around $84,000.

Alternatively, you can supplement your experience and existing education with a coaching credential. The one offered through the International Coach Federation is currently the most popular, and widely recognized as the global gold standard throughout the world. In addition to your credential, this path allows you to train through programs offered at a school like Coach Training World. There you learn not only how to coach others but how to start, run and develop your own business too.

This path is not only considerably faster (depending on your schedule), it's also much more cost-effective. Your tuition at an institute dedicated solely to coach training doesn't require things like student fees, textbooks and costs associated with a rapidly-expanding administration. For an Accredited Coach Training Program (ACTP) offered independent of a college or four-year university, expect to pay between $8,000 and

$20,000 for a Professional Certified Coach (PCC) training program.

In addition, unless you were born a business owner or are transitioning from one business into a coaching business, you'll want to plan on additional time, money and effort to learn the skills necessary to establish, market and develop your business. For some, that may look like an MBA. Others may opt to join the many business programs for coaches that cost anywhere from $2,000 to $50,000. A third option (for those on a shoestring budget) would be to allocate funds for marketing support as they become available.

In Chapter 7, I discussed the importance of attending an accredited coaching institute, one that supports your end goal to become a successful coach and entrepreneur. As you evaluate your school, ask about any additional costs that aren't included in the published prices. Unlike Coach Training World, many schools are not all-inclusive. Remember: there are multiple parts to becoming a professional coach, including mentor coaching, evaluations and testing, and practicum hours. These are in addition to your coach-specific training hours. Many schools charge extra.

Is the marketplace overcrowded?

Yes and no. Many people possess the innate desire to help others. Unfortunately, for one reason or another, far too few pursue the necessary avenues of professional training and development that would enable them to create reliable, sustainable change for their clients.

As you move forward in your career as a professional coach, you'll find yourself immersed with a number of untrained coaches. With this in mind, the marketplace indeed can feel overcrowded.

But stop and consider the number of people who take the shortcut of simply adding "Coach" to their title. Weed out these people (just like employers and clients are now doing) and the field becomes a lot less crowded. Through professional training and an ICF credential, that's exactly what you're doing: setting yourself apart from those who aren't truly capable of generating the same results you are.

Do I need to quit my job or leave my industry?

Where you make your difference is up to you. Many people become coaches as a way to shift into more meaningful work. But becoming a coach doesn't mean you have to change anything in your career.

Some professionals use coach training to advance within their chosen industry. Others use these skills to boost their resume and find similar work within other companies. And yes, some use coaching to completely reinvent their career and life at the same time.

Coaching skills are highly sought-after for leadership roles and by those who hold job titles such as career counselor, trainer or talent scout. Human Resources (HR) professionals also find coaching's tools and methodology to be of huge benefit in their day to day tasks. Additionally, I've seen many graduates who have been hired specifically for their coaching experience into roles they would not have been previously considered for. There are also those who are hired to create coaching programs for employees. These individuals enjoy the diversity of both coaching and curriculum design. And finally, let's not forget those who become coaches to take work in coaching firms.

In the training room, I often hear students offer up their well-thought-out transition plans. They focus on building a business while remaining fully employed. This strategy allows them to enjoy the comfort of a steady income while they grow their client base to equal or greater amounts of income. Others train to become a coach as a retirement option, staying active and engaged while making extra cash to fund trips and big purchases, or add to their nest egg. In truth, some who train never become full-time coaches. But the joy and fulfillment they receive by helping others part-time, not to mention the extra cash, is often benefit enough.

How do I convince my partner, husband, wife or family to support me on this venture?

Becoming a coach, like any other career pivot, is a major decision. And it's one that many people, especially those who love you and are close to you, may not understand at first. Spouses, partners and family members haven't had the benefit of your research or direct experience with coaching. You've invested time into checking out the coaching profession. They have not. Those closest to you can become concerned with the money aspect, especially when others may be potentially impacted. Again, this is a valid concern. But it's not one to be defeated by.

To gain their support, first recognize that with any kind of life-change others will be curious about how it's all going to play out in the end. This is doubly so when it comes to investing time and money into a new opportunity. Now think about anyone and everyone who will be impacted by your decision to go into coaching. Then consider what they might need to know to be comfortable and supportive of your decision.

Many of our students have shared that, as they were making their decision, they were met with skepticism. But it quickly dissolved when they presented their spouse, partner or parents with the research and curriculum required to certify. In fact, I can name numerous coaches who were able to "convert" their spouses after they saw the rewards that coaching can provide.

Among the most impressive were Erin and Jake. Erin came to coaching to enhance her capacity for online marketing services offered to a global client base. She and her husband owned the business together. After Erin completed her training, she cultivated noticeably greater results among her clients by focusing on the whole person. With her new skills and tools, she was able to shift the mindsets of her clients and assist them to get out of their own way of success. Referrals followed. Booked schedules ensued. And Jake was among the first to sign up for training the very next term.

How can I convince my employer to invest in my training?

It's not uncommon for employers to cover a portion if not the entire cost of coach training. If your company offers allowances for training and development, you'll want to align the company's need with what you'll be able to do for them after your training.

For example, one of our students was able to offer additional services to her company's client base, dramatically increasing revenue streams. Another was able to shift into a new role as manager and coach other employees, improving job-satisfaction among her group, as well as productivity. A third student used coaching skills to shift the company culture and created coaching programs for in-house use.

Similar to the top-of-mind problems you would be addressing for prospective clients, employers (especially big ones) have problems they'd like to resolve and opportunities they'd like to create. Speak to them about the value your coaching skills will bring to the company by demonstrating its application, benefits and proven success in similar ventures. Lastly, as an ICF member, you have access to pertinent research, which has the potential to add numbers to your cause.

Who should *not* become a coach?

Coaching isn't for everyone. If you love having all the answers and telling others how to do something, coaching probably isn't for you. Coaching is about engaging others in the change-making process. You help others figure it out for themselves, as opposed to simply giving them answers.

Coaching taps into your natural capacity for solving problems. It is applied to the creative, strategic process that's required to deeply and sustainably engage others to be at their best. The coaching process represents a subtle shift from doing the work for someone else to the more dynamic and collaborative process of problem-solving.

What are other resources people use to pay their tuition?

While some see student loans as an option to earn their degree at a university, this debt adds up quickly and can be incredibly hard to get out from under. Some coach training schools offer payment plans while others may have work programs. These can help alleviate the cost of the training, sometimes even delaying payment until you to begin coaching clients for pay (which can happen pretty quickly!).

Those unwilling to take on debt of any kind often look to foundation grants for assistance. Most local libraries can assist you with tracking down and applying for grants available to you. Many states also offer extended income support through unemployment divisions. Non-profits like Mercy Corps may provide financial resources and training. And others may qualify for additional benefits through the Vocational Rehabilitation and Employment (VR&E) program.

And of course, there's always family and friends. You'd be surprised how willing a grandmother, uncle or friend might be if they see a solid plan for your professional development – especially when it's for something you're truly excited about. We've seen everything from ex-boyfriends to anonymous lenders show up in support of our students. The key is to ask for help.

Training & Credentialing

How does online coach training work?

At Coach Training World, you have the option to join us live and in-person here in Portland, Oregon. The major benefit of taking the training at the institute is that students often form friendships and even business partnerships with one another due to the inclusivity and smaller, family-like training environment. But you don't have to. In fact, many people choose the online option to accommodate a busy schedule and offset the costs of travel. Keep in mind: you can always do both, attend a portion of the program online and the balance in-person. Over the next few years, we'll be spreading our wings into new locations, both in the United States and abroad.

We employ the latest technology to support students from all over the world. This extends our global community by allowing anyone with Internet access to join in and directly interact with each other. The beauty of this approach is that it's highly experiential. In a tech-based training program, you won't find a lot of endless lectures and sitting behind the computer. Instead, sessions are extremely interactive, involving students, mentors and teachers from a variety of distinct locations.

Breakout sessions are another aspect of online training. Here you participate in a small group format inside private conference rooms. Everything is recorded in the main room, with links provided for your review or scheduling convenience (if you happen to miss a session).

How does Whole Person Coaching work with other modalities?

Many coaching students originate from other fields of study. Common backgrounds range from communications, psychotherapy, social work and psychology degrees to certifications in Reiki, NLP, Theta healing, hypnotherapy, and tarot to name just a few. While these individuals possess subject matter knowledge and the ability to help their clients from their chosen perspective, they often lack a proven system that enables them to sustainably prosper from their passions and potential.

Coaching is the bridge between those two worlds. It forms a perfect partnership that advances their work and healing capacity while empowering their clients to achieve their best. The coaching process acts as a framework to evoke change in others while providing a firm base and financial business model for the coach. This enables them to capitalize on their many skills and unique knowledge to create a change process that guarantees results.

How does coaching differ from therapy and consulting?

A lot of confusion surrounds the difference between coaching and various types of therapy. Both represent valid ways to contribute to the well-being of an individual. But there are substantial differences between the two approaches.

Let's start by looking at the similarities.

Much like a therapist, a coach deeply listens. They are both deeply present to the client and their ideas, including struggles and triumphs. Both types of professionals also create a courageous space in which the client is encouraged to explore the intricacies of their life and any changes they want to make within it.

As a coach though, you focus on a process of self-discovery with your clients. You use thought-provoking questions to help them recognize and leverage their strengths and resources then self-create their desired end results. Unlike the therapist, upon whom their patients are often dependent for support, you build your client's capacity to be their own changemaker. A therapist is looking for interventions they can help the client make.

The true distinction lies in who is leading the change. In coaching, it's the client who leads the way.

A therapist may employ techniques like coaching within treatment. But in many cases, their role largely addresses clinically-diagnosable problems associated with mental health and trauma.

A therapist works with their clients to identify challenges through a diagnostic structure, typically based on the Diagnostic and Statistical Manual of Mental Disorders (DSM). Upon identifying a disorder, the therapist attempts to alleviate symptoms through counseling, specific protocols and, at times, prescription medications. The goal is typically a desired behavior or result – as defined by the therapist – with the client's well-being in mind. In contrast, a coach – and in particular you as a Whole Person Coach – does not rely on a pre-defined definition of normalcy. Coaching relationships do not involve the diagnosis or treatment of mental disorders as defined by the American Psychiatric Association. Nor is coaching a substitute for counseling, psychotherapy, psychoanalysis, mental health care or substance abuse treatment.

Instead, you encourage your clients to assess their lives though their own lens, drawing upon their unique experience and abilities to achieve success. Your primary goal is to inspire your clients to figure things out for themselves, supporting them through a holistic and richly-collaborative process. (It's worth noting that if you happen to have red hair, you're halfway there just by getting out of bed in the morning: we're natural muses. Botticelli's *The Birth of Venus*. Waterhouse's *The Lady of Shalott*. Degas' *Dancers*. I'm not making it up!)

Coaching is a professional client relationship in which you as the coach facilitate the creation or development of personal, professional or business goals – solely defined by your client. You then continue that support as they develop and carry out a strategy for achieving those goals. You recognize that the client is fully responsible for their physical, mental and emotional well-being. This includes the choices and decisions they make throughout the coaching process.

The future versus the past

Another major difference between the services you'll offer and that of a therapist is focus. As a coach, you work with your clients to create a preferred future while therapists endeavor to resolve the past.

Your process initiates on an upswing with a client who is inspired to create positive change in their life. The therapist begins in a place of struggle, and at times hopelessness, and must work toward the upswing before their future desires can be addressed.

Coaching is about moving forward. In fact, it's ALL about moving forward! It's future-focused. You are responsible for offering thought-provoking questions that invite your clients to think in new and improved ways as they work towards their desired outcome.

Coaching is a goal-centric, action-oriented process. It is based on an individual's ability to learn, change and transform their life. Through this transformational learning process, your clients discover where they really want to be by aligning with their values and virtues. They get there by becoming self-innovative. To achieve these objectives, you will focus on the present moment as it relates to the client creating their preferred future.

Each session is directed by what your client wants to focus on and what they want to accomplish.

In contrast, a therapist attempts to heal pain, dysfunction, or deep and often irresolvable conflict. The primary goal in this scenario is to resolve difficulties from the past that are hampering an individual's emotional functionality in the present, thereby improving overall psychological functioning.

Best of both disciplines

Many of the professionals previously mentioned, especially those classified as helping professionals or healers, are now incorporating the tools of coaching into their professional client services. These individuals seek to expand the way in which they work with their existing clients and attract a new type of client base into their practices. Others like Tara, who you met in Chapter 1, want to shift into work with different populations, servicing new and challenging needs while expanding their own experience as well.

Coaching versus consulting

Coaching is further distinguished from the advice-giving practices of experts and consultants in that it supports the individual (client) to seek guidance from within. In this way, people discover their own answers and develop the capacity to be continually resourceful through a self-innovative, self-directed process.

Consulting approaches vary widely. But it is generally assumed that the consultant or expert diagnoses problems, then advises and sometimes implements the most effective solutions from their point of view. These experts offer a tested, proven process that is unique and specialized in its application. This approach is almost always based solely on the consultant's particular expertise. As a result, the expert is offering their unique frame of reference, knowledge and skills. This is how he or she can suggest, diagnose, advise or solve a problem for an individual or system.

When you become a masterful change maker, you have the potential to offer your clients so much more. You gain the power to position individuals, groups or entire organizations to be self-innovative for the rest of their lives. By placing the responsibility for defining and achieving success in their court, you help them solve their problems and become more effective in life. Think about Kim, who you met in the Introduction. She challenged me to move past my sole focus on the corporate world that, at the time, wasn't ready for my vision of change. That's no longer the case. But by giving me a little shove (in my own direction, I might add), Kim invited me to redefine my future by ensuring I built my services on who I really was. (Thanks again, Kim!)

Before we move on, I want to highlight one additional trend. Like therapists, counselors and social workers, countless consultants are also turning to coaching as a reliable way to better support their clients. These individuals, operating within industries across the board, enjoy the way in which coaching engages and involves their clients in the process.

One such example is Dr. Kim Kutsch, a dentist who took coach training to amplify his patients' success. As Dr. Kutsch shared, traditional dental care is a process that manages immediate symptoms, not lasting health. Simply put, it tells the patient what to do and is more akin to a one-way form of communication rather than the partnership coaching strives to achieve.

"Classically, dentists are trained to tell patients what problems they see and then let them know what to do, giving them two or three options," Kutsch says. "But it's really about telling the patient – maybe educating a little bit about the option – but it's really about telling the patient what to do."

Kutsch went on to say that, regardless of the setting, a system of one-way diagnosis and treatment is ineffective. It often causes patients to lapse back into the same self-sabotaging behaviors for three very specific reasons.

It typically fails to account for:

1. What the patient wants for their health and why
2. Behaviors or lifestyle choices that need to be addressed to realize goals
3. A clear, sustainable, step-by-step plan to achieve greater and – most importantly – lasting health

In contrast, healthcare practitioners with coach training employ a process that involves and motivates the patient into behavior changes. Within this role, the consultant/coach becomes a support member for the patient, returning the power back to the individuals themselves.

What's the difference between the ICF and CCE?

Both of these credentialing organizations vet coaches and coach training programs. The biggest difference between credentials earned through the International Coach Federation (ICF) and the Center for Credentialing Education (CCE) is their recognizability.

An ICF credential is recognized the world over, with members currently operating in one hundred and thirty-eight countries. In contrast, CCE credential holders are currently in seventeen countries.

Additionally, whereas the ICF vets a coach's actual coaching skills, the CCE only does this on paper. They require coaches to be mentored, and their skills developed and evaluated throughout the coach training process to earn their credential.

That said, a CCE credential can be a benefit to some, especially working professionals who already hold advanced degrees or licenses. Becoming a Board Certified Coach (BCC) through the CCE may prove useful to you if you currently serve others as a therapist, counselor, social worker, psychologist or the like. In these instances, you can add coaching into your tool kit while applying your academic work experience toward the credential. This has the potential to save you time and money in the training process.

Do I need to pursue my ICF coaching credential?

There has been much debate on whether pursing an ICF coaching credential is necessary. I'll be the first to admit that, decades ago when the profession was just starting to get its legs, very few corporations, businesses and individuals even knew about the ICF and credentialed coaches. Today that's no longer true. Companies large and small use the ICF credential to vet coaches. Those with a higher level such as a Professional Certified Coach (PCC) or Master Certified Coach (MCC) receive the most attention.

But the ICF database isn't the only way companies vet and validate their future hires. Coaches are required to offer proof of their coaching capacity akin to a portfolio. Many must now submit sample coaching sessions to potential employers who are using the ICF's core competencies (or a comparable set of standards) to discern the skill level of their potential hire. These are skills you can only obtain by attending an ICF-accredited coach training program.

Having an ICF credential isn't just about demonstrating your commitment to coaching excellence and professional mastery. It's also a way to elevate yourself to the top of the list and get you into the doors of global companies and coaching firms. In this way, your credential functions like a professional resumé.

Because it's not just companies that use the credential to assess prospective coaches. Anyone who hires a coach can visit the ICF website and use their Credentialed Coach Finder to review an individual's credential status. Additionally, many advanced trainings such as Brené Brown's Daring Greatly and similar programs require attendees to hold an ICF credential. This ensures the participants are coming in at an adequate level of proficiency.

What is the ICF global network?

When you train to become a coach at an ICF accredited or approved program, you are invited to join the ICF global network. Available exclusively to professional coaches, it provides access to a network of like-minded individuals who are committed to traveling a similar path together.

The network gives you access that further develops your skills and working knowledge of the profession.

It includes current research, ongoing trainings, international and local conferences, and local chapters.

This type of collaboration and support has a long history among writers, painters, scientists, doctors and just about any group dedicated to bettering themselves and their practice. As individuals singularly committed to the development and betterment of our clients and the world around us, coaches are certainly no exception.

Starting Your Business

How do I get clients?

This is a question I get asked A LOT. Understandably so. At Coach Training World, we offer many courses and mentoring opportunities inside our CoachPreneur Academy. This ensures our students the most successful business launch possible. That being said, let's take a peek at what that process looks like.

The first thing to take into consideration is who your clients are. They are people who genuinely need your services and who will see you as a valid resource. They are not your family and friends. In marketing, we create what is called a client avatar. It's a clear, concise description of your ideal client. Your avatar is formed by identifying the types of people you want to serve from a demographic and psychographic perspective.

For example, are you most interested in helping professional women of color climb the corporate ladder? Or maybe you want to help pro golfers who are struggling to take first place. Knowing who you want to help and what they want to accomplish or overcome is your first step. It's a step you'll learn inside a business incubator like CoachPreneur Academy.

Next you'll learn how to position your services to magnetize your ideal clients to you. Inside a program like ours, you discover the fastest, most effective ways to position, brand and successfully market yourself, both online and off. This stage walks you through the process of creating a solid brand. It's worth noting that it doesn't have to be fancy. However, your brand must clearly impart to your clients that you are the one they need most.

You will then use your brand to attract more and more people by showing up in the world as only you can. For some, this is in the form of blogging, speaking and podcasting. Others volunteer, lead workshops or create group presentations. And still others leverage their creative spark to write a short book or create a video series – you'd be amazed at the number of authors that got their start at CTW.

If you are newer to entrepreneurship or worry about asking for what you are worth, you may need to address the limiting money beliefs or those centered on visibility that are currently holding you back. If you suffer from stage fright, you're in good company – I was at the head of that particular line long before you. But marketing can be a lot of fun. Like coaching, it's about having a "conversation" and "interactions" with others in a variety of media forms. These conversations generate a connection, interest and eventually an investment in someone's future.

Think of marketing as an exploratory coaching session, one in which you're focused on being in service to your ideal clients. Suddenly the marketing process gets a whole lot easier. Besides, whether you realize it or not, you are already a natural at attracting people and selling them on a preferred future!

When can I quit my day job?

When the time is right. Only you know your tolerance for uncertainty. If you've got the financial resources to cover you for a couple years, enabling you to focus exclusively on establishing your business, then statistically you'll probably be okay. But again, this is only an estimate. Your financial responsibilities are the big determining factor here. And don't forget to allow for unforeseen emergency expenses (medical bills, car or house repairs, etc.).

Before you jump ship (and I know it's hard to wait, especially if you are more than done with your day job), bear in mind how the loss of your immediate income may increase your stress levels. Fear can be ignited when our bank account begins to drop without a clear view of the next source of income.

Yet rest assured, your good efforts will pay off. In time, you too will be off someone else's payroll and onto your own business success. Take courage in the fact that there is never a moment in your life that is 'all or nothing'. You can always begin your transition and start a business by adding one client at a time.

What if I'm a new business owner?

First off: good for you! If you're a new business owner, you are in a premium position to learn the latest, most effective marketing and business strategy tools ever designed.

With the ease-of-use inherent in most software platforms these days, you don't need a bunch of technical know-how to get your message out there either. You can tap into global audiences available through Facebook, Twitter and LinkedIn to get your message to those who are actively seeking people just like you. If blogging, podcasting or video-streaming is your thing, there are no shortage of platforms on which you can broadcast content and get known.

To further expedite your success, I always recommend partnering with a business mentor. Ideally this will be someone who has successfully traveled the entrepreneurial world as a coach. This person will know the road well. They can help you navigate the various phases and challenges of being a solopreneur, especially when it comes to selling yourself and your coaching products and services to others. You'll often find them in a coach training program that includes business development and marketing courses like CTW's CoachPreneur Academy. These individuals are not only professional coaches, they're also successful businesspeople. They've discovered the best ways to capitalize on their experience and are more than willing to share it with those who are just starting out. Some are simply coaches looking to 'pay it forward'. Others are coaches who have dedicated themselves to coaching other coaches to success.

To slightly reiterate what I said in the opening chapters of this book, it's essential for coaches who plan on becoming business owners to allow for schooling in coach training as well as the business of change. Starting a coaching business is easiest and most successful when you study the skills and tools of a coaching modality in combination with the tools and strategies of a committed business owner.

How long will it take to become profitable?

Coaching is a viable profession and business endeavor. But training to become a professional coach and launching your coaching business is not something that happens overnight.

Except for a winning lottery ticket, I challenge you to name a single profession that immediately places you at the top of the game. And quite frankly, would you want to be elevated that quickly? Coaching, like baking, music, dentistry, and the practice of law, is a learning experience. Though you bring all of who you are to the business of coaching, you begin as a novice. As you coach clients, you gain experience (fewer professions provide better or more profitable on-the-job training). From there, your success is as great or as modest as you desire.

Change is difficult. Changing others is even more challenging. That's why you'll want the skills, tools and experience gained through a professional training school and gold-standard pedigree such as an ICF credential. As we discussed in Chapter 2, your reputation hinges on your ability to change others in a sustainable way. This is especially true for those of us who become Whole Person Coaches. Our entire business model is centered on holistic results that originate within the individual client. No results, no referrals. Worse still: no repeat business. This places you in the unenviable position of constantly having to market and sell yourself instead of enjoying the rewards of a business that takes care of you.

Circling back to your timeline to success, consider famous people like Tony Robbins, Oprah and Martha Beck. They took years to build their global presence. In all honesty, you won't transform into a millionaire overnight. It probably won't even happen in the first year (some do, but it's not the norm). But if you are passionate about generating a profit, and are driven toward creating those numbers in your business, you are unlimited as a professional coach.

You'll find yourself at the center of the snowball effect. The passionate drive of yours will not only keep you motivated, it will also magnetize others to you. It's captivating to be around someone who is unstoppable in the pursuit of their dreams. And as you move forward and build your personal tribe, what started as a tiny snowball now has the power of an avalanche. In short, the more devoted you are, the faster you'll profit. The exact time it will take truly depends on you.

Most new businesses take two to three years to get established. But I know plenty of coaches (myself included) who leveraged their existing connections and professional relationships to pursue full-time coaching work almost immediately.

What if I'm not famous or don't know very many people?

If you've watched any of the modern online coaches, you've probably heard people talk about the importance of growing your mailing list.

Some coaches go to extreme lengths to build an email list consisting of tens of thousands of individuals. But I'd like to introduce you to a different perspective: don't count your prospects by how many are on the list but rather by the quality of the leads you have. Your email list can be as large as Amazon's, but you'll never book clients if you're marketing to people who are not your ideal demographic. This is true whether you're selling an offer worth $100 or $10,000.

Decide on the number of clients you want then build your list from there. And keep in mind: list-building isn't limited to online opt-in forms. You can grow your audience any time you speak or network with others. Most coaches start their businesses with lists as small as twenty to one hundred people. As few as ten clients who are interested in what you offer can provide a great start to your business.

How many products/programs do I need before I launch my coaching business?

Zero. Rare is the coach who launches their business with products or even coaching programs. In fact, many highly successful coaches work privately, first witnessing the power of coaching in action. From this experience and perspective, they create results-oriented programs and products with their ideal clients in mind. In time, you too can rock the Internet with your digital products and online coaching programs if that is part of your coaching business model.

What if I can't devote forty hours a week to this?

The only person creating a timeline for your business is you. If you can't devote forty hours a week to your coaching business right now, then you're like just about everyone else I know. Instead of getting stuck in an 'all or nothing' mentality, decide what you can commit to. Many people transition from their current career into their coaching business as part of a steady, well thought-out process.

Take Tina for example. Tina had worked a nine-to-five job for nearly two decades at a large residential and commercial painting company. She had established herself into a secure position that was hers for 'as long as she wanted it'. It was a rarity in this day and age of nonexistent loyalty among big employers. Yet somehow Tina could never shake the feeling that something was missing.

She decided to take Monday off every week and replace the lost income through coaching. Tina began by offering workshops that allowed her to work for two hours on that one day a week yet still generate the same amount of income she would've made at her day job. Building on this model, she slowly transitioned from her day job into her own business.

Most people don't believe they can ask for a day off from work. And there are probably some who can't. But do you really want to work in a place like that? For those who might have a little more leeway to take time but are afraid to ask for it, there are many ways to get around simply taking the day off. Sick days and paid leave days are two easy strategies.

Plus, if you aren't losing income, you can use the time worry-free to develop your business. How great would that be: getting paid to pursue something you love! Sure, it might feel as though you're trading your precious "paid days off" for your business. But you are actually creating a business that will reward you with ten times the number of free days, a schedule you set for yourself, and a boss who never says no (you!).

Don't wait. You need to start somewhere, and every moment counts.

Other Questions

Does coaching really work?

Yes, it does. But don't take my word for it. Check out any of the thousands of people who have personally and professionally changed their lives through coaching. Even though the profession is only in its fourth decade, research reveals "coaching has significant positive effects on performance and skills, well-being, coping, work attitudes, and goal-directed self-regulation," according to a recent study by researchers at the University of Amsterdam.[1]

The study, entitled "Does Coaching Work? - A Meta-analysis on the Effects of Coaching on Individual Level Outcomes in an Organizational Context," went on to cite coaching as "an effective tool for improving the functioning of individuals in organizations." Taking their stance a step further, the researchers also stated, "it is now time to shift attention from the question 'does it work?' to 'how does it work?'."

Coaching is here to stay. Recent industry figures estimate coaching services and products account for over $2 billion in annual revenue globally. An independent analysis recently found that as much as $1 billion of that total may be in the United States alone. Companies and individuals are spending good money each year and

---

1 Theeboom, Tim, Bianca Beersma, and Annelies E.M. van Vianen. 2013. "Does coaching work? A meta-analysis on the effects of coaching on individual level outcomes in an organizational context." *The Journal of Positive Psychology* 9 (1): 1-18.

returning to professionally trained coaches for help with areas in addition to their initial problem. That would be a lot of money, time and faith wasted each year if it "didn't work." Wouldn't you agree?

What if my life isn't perfect?

None of us come to the coaching profession fully-formed. We all have our personal roadblocks that are amplified by the voice of doubt. No one is perfect. But this is the trap so many potential coaches fall into: they give in to the misconception that they have to show up with perfect lives or provide firsthand knowledge for every conceivable question. This is false.

To become a professional (and valued) coach, you learn the process through professional training and mentoring. You then tailor this process by incorporating your life experience and expertise. This is similar to what you'll soon be doing for your clients – you are a process expert. You facilitate a highly creative process that supports your clients to do the work needed to get from where they are to where they truly want to be.

As a professional coach, you aren't selling your life. You're selling your capacity to help someone change theirs. That's why it is so important to get professionally trained. It gives you tools backed by a proven system. This process not only trains you what to look for, it shows you the most effective and holistic ways to help that individual. More importantly, it frees you from having to rely on your perspective and experience alone, as many untrained individuals and even renowned consultants do. Instead, you are empowered to leverage your knowledge inside a full system designed to evoke change.

What if someone in the coaching industry knows more than me?

I hate to break this to you, but you could toss this book in almost any direction and hit someone who knows more about something than you. There will always be someone who started sooner, took a different development path, or simply has an interest in something they dedicated themselves to. In the same way, you know more about some things than they do. But that's not really the issue here.

Thoughts like 'What if I don't know enough?' or 'What if I don't have a fully-formed answer?' are nothing more than the voice fear speaking. It's part of the comparison contract that comes from growing up in a world that's taught us we are only valuable in relation to others and when we have answers.

The beauty of the Whole Person Coaching process is its unique way of leveraging both your wisdom and that of your clients inside a highly creative and effective change-making process. Whole Person Coaching is designed to produce results regardless of your level of experience with the subject at hand. This facet also enables change to spread exponentially throughout your life and the lives of your clients.

Never be put off by how little you know on a given subject. With practice, you'll learn to get to the core of the problem through a reliable step-by-step process. You'll become a change master in no time, pursued by a strong following of raving fans and referrals.

What other questions do you have?

Did I miss your question? No worries. I've got you covered. Feel free to email me anything on your mind. Or if you prefer a more personal method of communication, call us directly.

www.coachtrainingworld.com

info@coachtrainingworld.com

1-888-660-5588

Appendix

The Scientific and Psychological Roots of Whole Person Coaching

It's important to know the foundational roots of a coaching method. When working with the "whole person," you embody a rich tool kit and strong scientific background.

The Whole Person Coaching method and its accompanying tools provide you with insight drawn from the wisdom and best practices of multiple disciplines. They embrace research and theory from the following fields:

Mindfulness

Comprised of two central components: awareness and acceptance. Awareness is the ability to notice your thoughts, feelings and bodily sensations. It can be expanded to include deeper thought processes such as noticing the lens from which you see yourself and others and the story from which you live. Acceptance is where the non-judgmental component of Whole Person Coaching comes into play. This secondary element encourages us to acknowledge our thoughts and experience without labeling them as positive or negative. Doing so makes it possible to explore what lives within the shadows as well and the light, and for our fullest and highest potential to be realized.

Positive Psychology

The study of specific strengths and virtues that lead to success for individuals and organizations. Based on the work of Martin Seligman, it assumes people want to lead meaningful lives and works to enhance their experience by cultivating the best from that which is currently within them.

Neuro Linguistic Programing (NLP)

The study of human excellence through the development of an individual's behavioral competence and flexibility. Neuro meaning mind, lingustic meaning language, and the programming residing within the mind's database that can be updated. Originated by Richard

Bandler and John Grinder, NLP uses self-discovery and the exploration of identity as a framework for human experience. It extends beyond the individual to family, as well as local and global communities.

Narrative Psychology

The branch of psychology dedicated to how we are shaped and adapt to life's experiences through story and language. Explored in depth by Theodore R. Sarbin, this discipline uses an individual's observed stories, as well as those garnered from others, to interpret human conduct.

Emotional Intelligence (EI)

The ability of an individual to leverage available emotional information to guide their thinking and subsequent behavior. Though not the first to coin the term, Emotional Intelligence is largely attributed to psychologist and author Daniel Goleman, whose 1995 book detailed the importance of an individual recognizing their feelings, as well as those of others, to adapt to specific situations and achieve goals more effectively.

Whole Person Learning

A form of transformative learning that enables an individual to incorporate all aspects of their persona (intellectual, social, emotional, physical and spiritual) by viewing them in context with the world around them. The ultimate goal is to facilitate improved relationships and functioning by focusing on the interconnected, interdependent nature of life.

Meta-Learning

The understanding of one's own thought and learning processes. Originally proposed by Donald B. Maudsley, it is dedicated to increasing awareness of habits related to perception, inquiry, learning, and growth that an individual has internalized over the course of their life.

Somatic Psychology

Dedicated to somatic experience, or how we experience the physical world internally and move in the world externally. Taking cues from yoga and even ballet and modern dance, somatic psychology is a holistic approach that centers on the mind/body interface and how this interaction influences our thoughts, behaviors, actions and interactions with others.

Archetypal Psychology

The use of psychology to see, image and envision what it means to be human by accessing the deepest patterns of psychic functioning, often referred to as "soul." Carl Jung viewed archetypes as archaic yet universal representations originating from within the collective unconscious. As inherited potentials, they can be seen as complementary to human instinct. These images become actualized in our behavior and interactions.

Expressive Arts

The use of personal creativity as a starting point for discovery, self-reflection, understanding and change. Expressive arts is a thought-provoking process widely used to ignite one's imagination and intuition. It is also highly effective at facilitating an in-depth examination of the body, feelings, emotions and an individual's thought process. Additionally, it is frequently used to create balance in the brain hemispheres and a more holistic outlook in general.

Developmental Psychology

The branch of psychology concerned with how and why we change over the course of our lives. Initially concerned primarily with infants and children, the discipline has since expanded to encompass the full lifespan of the individual, tackling broad topics such as motor skills and executive functions, as well as moral understanding and self-concept. By viewing the change in an individual over time, developmental psychology attempts to decode the influence of nature and nurture.

Adult Attachment Theory

Describes the impact of long- and short-term interpersonal relationships among adults, primarily centered on friendships, emotional affairs and romantic attachments. Originally developed by British psychoanalyst John Bowlby, the theory states that the same motivational system solidifying the bond between parent and child also influences relationships among adults within emotionally-intimate relationships. Therefore, the way in which we approach our relationships today is largely dependent upon the style of attachment developed early in life (secure, ambivalent, avoidant or disorganized).

Interpersonal Neurobiology (IPNB)

An interdisciplinary field incorporating a range of practices, such as anthropology, biology, computer science, linguistics, psychiatry and sociology (among many others). The primary aim is to uncover commonalities in the human experience. Pioneered by Daniel J. Siegel, M.D., IPNB burst onto the scene years ago with revelations on how the brain develops within relationships. The discipline coined the term "social brain." It provides the key to coaching and understanding how we can best support our clients. More significantly, it explains the deep web of influence that exists between relationships and motivation. From this starting point, Siegel ventured on to mindfulness, developing his MindSight Approach and linking it back to IPNB. Siegel is not the only researcher involved with Interpersonal Neurobiology however. Other significant contributors include psychologists Dr. Louis Cozolino, who focused on the social brain, and Dr. Allan Schore who is known for his work with modern attachment and early right-brain development.

About Us

FEROSHIA KNIGHT is an ICF Master Certified Coach, educator and the creator of Whole Person Coaching. For nearly 30 years, she has successfully championed individuals and organizations throughout the world toward holistic, sustainable development.

As founder of Coach Training World in Portland, Oregon, Feroshia

Photo courtesy of wagtomyheart.com

has created one of the most holistic, heart-centered and well-respected coach training institutes in the United States. She is also an internationally-known motivational speaker, entrepreneur, consultant, coach and author. Connect with her at: www.coachtrainingworld.com, and on www.facebook.com/coachtrainingworld.

RYAN MAY is an author and freelance copywriter with clients in 17 countries. Throughout the past decade, he has written extensively for products and services in more than 30 specialized industries. Connect with him at: www.forgedink.com, and on Twitter @forgedink.